M000247554

Living by the Light of the Moon

2021 Moon Book

Beatrex Quntanna

Copyright ©2020 by Beatrex Quntanna

All Rights Reserved. No part of this book may be reproduced or transmitted in any form or by any means without the written permission of the publisher, except for the inclusion of brief quotations in a review.

ISBN 978-0-578-79461-7

Printed in the United States of America

ART ALA CARTE PUBLISHING

760-944-6020

beatrex@cox.net

www.beatrex.com

This book is dedicated to
Jennifer Masters
for her ability to turn
my words into art and design.
Thank you, Jennifer.

Acknowledgments

Thank you Jennifer Masters for the cover art and your ability to capture the inspirational theme with your magical graphic art. Additionally, for your dedication to refinement on all levels in the book and beyond. Michelenne Crab for the daily Tibetan Numerology intentions that inspire and direct us to make the most of each day. Inspiring us to live in harmony with the universal timing of all things. Jill Estensen for the astrological calculations for the entire year. Also, for sharing aspects from *Dimensional Astrology* that add an innovative approach to the Sabian Symbols, experiencing the degrees and the polarity that they create for each moon phase. Special thanks to Kaliani Devinne for contributing all new goddess profiles that correspond to each moon cycle and the moon charts this year. Candice Covington for her approach to the elements. Ann Meyer for the freedom affirmations from Teaching of the Inner Christ. Melinda Pajak and Terri Strathairn for being the overlighting divas and adding the finishing touches. Felicia Bond for bringing the goddesses to life in Moon Class on zoom each month. Soon, Felicia will bring her goddess teachings to Blue Moon Academy.

Special thanks to Nykole Coombs, Melinda Pajak, and LeahRose for hosting Moon Class on Zoom, giving me the pleasure to continue teachings during Covid-19.

Last but not least, a special thank you to the countless students who come to Moon Class – without you this teaching would not exist!

Production Team

Art Direction, Book Design, Cover Art, and Video Editing (*How to Use the Moon Book* video class series)
Jennifer Masters
www.JenniferMastersCreative.com

Daily Tibetan Numerology
Michelenne Crab
www.mydailytarotcard.com

Astrological Calculations, Sabian Symbols and *Dimensional Astrology*
Jill Estensen
intuvision@roadrunner.com

Goddess Profiles
Kaliani Devinne
www.SelenityMoon.com

Book and Calendar Editors
Melinda Pajak and Terri Strathairn

Sky Power Yoga
Jennifer "Tashi" Vause, R.Y.T.
yogatashi@yahoo.com   www.BlueMoonAcademy.com

Video Production (online classes with Beatrex)
Robert Simmons
858-449-1749   www.BlueMoonAcademy.com

Table of Contents

About the Art 6

The Importance of Cycles 7

How To Use This Book 8

January 12
    Capricorn New Moon   14
    Leo Full Moon   22

February 30
    Aquarius New Moon   32
    Virgo Full Moon   40

March 48
    Pisces New Moon   50
    Libra Full Moon   58

April 66
    Aries New Moon   68
    Scorpio Full Moon   76

May 84
    Taurus New Moon   86
    Sagittarius Full Moon – Lunar Eclipse   94

June 102
    Gemini New Moon – Solar Eclipse   104
    Capricorn Full Moon   112

July 120
    Cancer New Moon   122
    Aquarius Full Moon   130

August 138
    Leo New Moon   140
    Aquarius Full Moon   148

September 156
    Virgo New Moon   158
    Pisces Full Moon   166

October 174
    Libra New Moon   176
    Aries Full Moon   184

November 192
    Scorpio New Moon   194
    Taurus Full Moon – Lunar Eclipse   202

December 210
    Sagittarius New Moon – Solar Eclipse   212
    Gemini Full Moon   220

Appendices 229

About the Author 236
    Online Classes With Beatrex   237
    Other Publications By Beatrex   239

About the Art

Finding the theme of 2021 in the midst of experiencing 2020 proved to be difficult! I had this image of the Goddess Hecate standing at the crossroads in my mind's eye pretty early on in the creative process. My curiosity ignited, I began my research on her. During this time many other ideas came and went, but at last a consensus: Hecate at the crossroads.

So, I created this digital graphic in less than two days. I actually tried to keep it more simplistic since time was of the essence, but once I began she took on a life of her own. For the overall design I was guided by one of the main qualities of the Tibetan Numerology of the year: movement. Everything from the typeface I chose to the zodiac symbols I created, I asked myself, does it show movement?

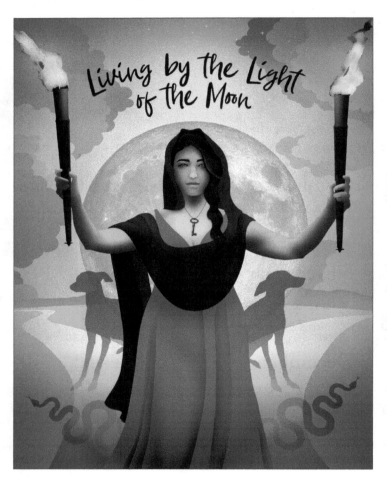

Hecate is a Titan from Ancient Greece, but there is evidence to suggest she is older and may originate from parts east, possibly Mesopotamia.

She is a lunar goddess of mystery and of magical practice, presiding over the phases of life, and of birth and death, protector of the vulnerable.

The crossroads is symbolic of an important choice to be made along the journey ... a decision, a turning point, a rebirth, creativity. Hecate is sometimes depicted as having three heads or three bodies standing back-to-back, holding torches to light the way. In Southern Europe a crossroads was usually three roads converging to a point (like a capital "Y"). Thus, she sees in all directions simultaneously. At the center of the crossroads is both all roads and no roads. It's a liminal space, a boundary, a place in between. From this place, all directions hold potential. As the Goddess of liminal spaces she is called upon for guidance.

Her torches are symbolic of her leadership, guiding initiates on their journey, and guiding the souls of the dead to where they need to go. It is Hecate who guides Demeter in her search for Persephone, and becomes Persephone's guide and companion in the underworld.

The fire on her torches symbolizes the light of the Moon and represents life and her connection to the life cycle. It also symbolizes the knowledge and wisdom gained through the process of initiation. Initiation is a symbolic liminal space, a threshold, a death and rebirth, a transformation borne of an experience.

She carries the key to unlock the mysteries and has the freedom to cross boundaries, the door or gateway being another symbol of a liminal space, a threshold that is neither inside nor outside, a place in between.

Dogs are sacred to Hecate. They are her companions and her heralds; barking dogs announce her presence. They are also a symbol of protection. She is also associated with snakes and serpent deities, symbols of healing and magic.

This is merely scratching the surface of this multifaceted goddess. For more about her, I recommend *Circle for Hekate - Volume I: History & Mythology* by Sorita d'Este and *Hekate Liminal Rites: A historical study of the rituals, spells and magic of the Torch-bearing Triple Goddess of the Crossroads* by Sorita d'Este and David Rankine.

—Jennifer Masters
Artist, Illustrator, Graphic Designer

The Importance of Cycles

The Moon is the keeper of the secrets of life and its cycles set the stage for successful living. Beatrex has developed a valuable collection of knowledge about how to use the cycles of the Moon to enhance the quality of your life. This workbook reveals those secrets and supports you in implementing them. Each cycle offers a different combination of light energy to give you the chance to grow harmoniously into wholeness. Following the luminaries, the Sun and the Moon, through the zodiac and noting the cycles of illumination and reflection can bring you to a deeper creative experience of life. The Moon is the great cosmic architect—the builder and the dissolver of form. Full Moons are about dissolving and New Moons are about building. This workbook will assist you in knowing what and when to build and what and when to dissolve with activities for each cycle of the Moon throughout 2021.

Life, at the highest spiritual level, moves beyond time and uses cycles to increase your ability to actualize your full potential. Cycles are in charge of your personal development; while time is in charge of the change in direction that happens when you evolve by trusting in divine timing. This workbook synthesizes techniques that allow for the power of development and direction to occur in the entire spectrum of wholeness. Each Zodiac sign holds the knowledge necessary to integrate an aspect of yourself to become whole. As the Moon and the Sun travel around our planet each month, a different aspect of self-development is presented to you via the zodiac sign constellation that it visits.

This year, 2021, begins with major choice points between adaptability and survival, power and empowerment, and progress and resistance. According to Tibetan Numerology, the number 5 is the ruler for the year and it takes us to the umbrella energy of the planet Mars; action, change, and variety. The year will ask us to define our action either by the 2nd-dimensional point of power, "I see, I want, and I *take*", better known as the Law of the Jungle; or by the 6th-dimensional point of power which is *empowerment*, a concept of change that comes from setting intention rather than using brute force to accomplish the goal, also called progress.

Most of the year, with the Mars and number 5 influence, is all about change, action, power, progress, adjustment, and adaptability—all in service to the ultimate goal of this decade, *transformation*. The many crossroads we will encounter this year will bring us to the altar of change which will create many choices with unresolved outcomes. The crossroads will motivate adaptability, adjustment, power, and empowerment setting us up with multi-level choice points. Adaptability will keep us in the motion required to make the best of the year. Charles Darwin wrote, "It is not the strongest of the species that survives, nor the most intelligent that survives. It is the one that is most adaptable to change that survives." This multitude of choice points and many crossroads will ask us to make choices beyond our perceived survival issues.

So, we begin the second year of the transformational decade with Uranus, the ruler of our future, which is retrograde until the 13th of the month. This thirteen-day period gives us chance to reset ourselves from the unifying factor of the year 2020 and set a new course of action in 2021, called "The Year of Adaptability." The power of Mars' action, along with Uranus' future focus, will be bringing a new speed factor to the docile, slow-moving tempo of the earth. This speed ratio will assist the earth in the healing that is necessary for the transformation required.

How to Use This Book

When the Moon is New

When the Moon is new, it is in the same sign as the Sun. This unites the power of the magnetic and the dynamic fields that are in perfect resonance for manifesting. This is a potent time to make your desires known by writing your manifesting list. Use the astrological theme to write your list like a child who is writing to Santa Claus. Be comfortable with extending your list's boundaries beyond what you believe is possible by thinking: *This, or something better than this, comes to me in an easy and pleasurable way for the good of all concerned.* Then light a candle and read your list out loud. Place it under an eight-sided mirror and put your candle on top of the mirror. Make sure to use a candle in glass—a votive or seven-day candle—to protect from fire. Place outside in the moonlight or in a special place in your home. Let the candle burn out. By the time the candle burns out, your list is in operation.

When the Moon is Full

It is time to release and set yourself free when the Moon is full and in direct opposition to the Sun. This polarity dissolves anything that stands in the way of your personal recalibration. Sixty hours before a full moon you may experience tension as the Sun and the Moon oppose each other. Learn to understand the opposite natures without feeling the need to separate them. Find the middle ground so that you are not manipulated by polarity as the integration of opposites creates the unity that creates harmony.

The polarity themes are on each full moon's page. Use the astrological theme to inspire you to renew your life by writing a releasing list. Light a candle and read your list out loud. Place your releasing list under a circle-shaped mirror and put your candle on top of the mirror. Make sure to use a candle in glass—a votive or seven-day candle—to protect from fire. Place outside in the moonlight or in a special place in your home. Let the candle burn out. When

your candle is finished burning, your list is in operation. Empty space allows manifestation to occur. Before writing your list you might want to look over the full moon cycle's trigger points to see if there is anything you need to let go of first. Remember recalibration allows you to live without resistance.

Your Time Zone

All times listed in the book are local to the Pacific time zone. Add or subtract hours accordingly to adjust times for your time zone. It is best to do your manifestation and freedom ceremonies at the specific times noted.

These Sections Will Help You To Live By the Light of the Moon

Planetary Highlights

This section explains the planets and how they will affect your life each month. It does not contain all of the aspects; it simply highlights points of interest that promote personal growth during each month. If you are interested in more study, take an astrology class. If you are an astrologer and want more information, we have provided a chart for each moon phase for your convenience.

The Monthly Calendar

This section provides you with a monthly overview and keeps you connected to the lunar, solar, and planetary cycles. It lets you know when the Moon is void-of-course, when it moves into a new sign, when the Sun and planets change signs, and when a planet goes retrograde or stationary direct (shown by the ℞ and ⅍ symbols). The calendar also has the Tibetan Numerology of the Day, along with an affirmation, to help you align with the energy and set your intentions for the day.

Void Moon

When the Moon is void-of-course, it has made its last major aspect in a sign and stays void until it enters the next sign. When the Moon is void-of-course, you will see the icon V/C on the calendar. This is not a good time to start new projects, relationships, or to take trips, unless you intend to never follow through. When the Moon ☽ enters a new sign, you will see this arrow → It will be followed by the symbol for the new sign and the time that the Moon enters it.

Super-Sensitivity ▲

This happens when the Moon travels across the sky, hits the center of the galaxy, and connects with a fixed star. When this happens the atmosphere becomes chaotic. An extra amount of energy pours down in a spiral at a very fast speed making it difficult to focus. This fragility can make you depressed, anxious, dizzy, and accident-prone. It is a good idea to keep your thought process away from this energy. This is global, not personal.

Low-Vitality ▼

This happens when the Moon is directly opposite the center of the galaxy. When this fixed-star opposition occurs, the Earth becomes very fragile and gets depleted. This leads to exhaustion in our physical bodies and is a sign for us to nurture ourselves by resting. The depletion can create Earth changes. Endings can also happen and resistance to these completions will bring on exhaustion. Best to detach and let go.

The Sun

Each month you will see the icon for the Sun ☉ with an arrow → indicating when the Sun enters a new sign. When the Sun changes signs, the climate of energy takes on a new theme for your personal development. Look for the Sun icon, with an arrow followed by an astrological sign, to indicate sign change and time.

Planets

Planets also change signs and move in retrograde and direct motions. Retrograde planets are next to the date in each day's box followed by retrograde icon ℞. In the middle of each box is information about planetary changes of time and direction.

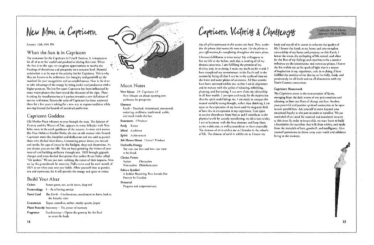

Goddesses

When the Moon enters a new zodiac sign, a changing of guardians occurs. Deep within each sign lives a goddess who is the keeper of this cyclical domain. This archetype's assignment is to hold the space for an aspect of wholeness to actualize.

Build Your Altar

An altar is an outer focus for inner work. Esoteric coordinates such as Tarot cards, flowers, colors, gemstones, fragrances, and numerology are provided as an enhancement to better assist you in working with each moon phase. Perhaps you are working on a love theme; you might want to add six hearts, six flowers, and six gemstones on your altar with your manifesting or freedom list, mirror, and candle. The coordinating Tarot card can be used as a visual activation. Flowers, colors, and gemstones accent your intentions. The fragrance provides a special connection to Spirit. You may want to burn candles of this scent, spritz your aura or your altar with the fragrance, or simply sniff the fragrance to awaken your olfactory system. Go to www.beatrex.com for moon mists, mirrors, and candle wraps.

The Elements

Each moon cycle has a primary element (earth, air, fire or water), attached to the astrological sign to which it is assigned, that brings you more awareness of what to work on during the cycle.

"I" Statements

These statements align the Self with the characteristics of the astrological sign and the house the sign lives in.

Body – Mind – Spirit

Each astrological sign rules a body part, a mental trait or attitude, and a spiritual condition. This section is provided to increase understanding of the tendencies and patterns that are activated during the moon transit.

Umbrella Energy

Each house the Moon moves through brings a focus for that moon as a baseline for self-development during the moon phase.

Karmic Awakenings

Every once in a while the chart for the Moon will show an intercepted astrological sign in a house on the chart. This indicates that a karmic pattern is in operation on that day.

Choice Points: Action – Non-action – Potential

Dimensional Astrology presents us with a prescribed action for each of the 360-degrees on the astrology wheel. The object of Dimensional Astrology is to depolarize and neutralize. The degree of the Moon is described to better enhance your understanding of the phase and its effects on you and your world. The wisdom comes with the actualization of potential; when we experience and combine the opportunity and the challenge without judgment.

Sabian Symbols

Each degree in the chart is identified with a symbolic language that speaks to your unconscious awareness and leads you to a new potential. The Sabian Symbols were given birth in California in 1925 by Mark Edmond Jones, a noted astrologer, working with gifted clairvoyant Elsie Wheeler. The symbol for the degree of the Moon is described to better enhance your understanding of the phase and its effects on you and your world.

Victories and Challenges

These are sets of affirmations designed to say out loud during a specific moon cycle to determine a motivational tone for your self-discovery. After saying all of them out loud, you will know which statement applies to you. Circle the one that is yours and use it as a personal mantra daily during the moon phase.

Victory List

Acknowledge what you have overcome. Keep this list active throughout this cycle. Honoring victories allows you to accept success.

Tarot

Sometimes it is good support to get another opinion on how you are doing with each cycle. Included for each moon is a new section where you can pull a Tarot card, using just the Major Arcana cards, and get more information on your process from a Universal perspective. There is a glossary of meanings in the appendix. For a more in-depth look at the Tarot, go to *www.beatrex.com/the-book-store* and look for Tarot: A Universal Language by Beatrex Quntanna.

Manifesting List

Write down what you want to create and manifest in your life.

Clearing the Slate

The first step to accepting freedom is to clear the slate from trigger points that need to be released as we head into the full moon cycle. Each section is filled with trigger points that are specific to the astrological sign where the Moon resides. See if any of them feel familiar. Acknowledge what's familiar and then follow the instructions by writing down what happened and perform Ho'oponopono, the Hawaiian forgiveness ritual. For example, a negative trigger point for Leo is impatience. When you find yourself being impatient, write down the circumstances or journal about it. Then, looking in the mirror, apologize to yourself, ask for forgiveness, have gratitude for yourself with thanks that you could see your impatience as a trigger, and then return to love.

Gratitude List

Keep this list active throughout this cycle. This will bring you to a level of completion so that a new cycle of opportunity can occur in your life.

Releasing List

What do you need to let go of in order to set yourself free?

List Ideas

Use these ideas to jump start your own lists. Let your imagination take off from here.

The Astro Wheel

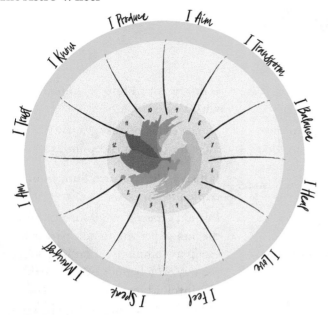

Western astrological charts are placed within a circle or wheel. The wheel is a picture of the sky from a particular place and time on Earth. It is divided into 12 parts called "houses." Each house deals with a particular area of life. Key concepts for each house are written outside the wheel. Compare the wheel in the book to your very own chart and discover the theme that you will be living personally during the moon phase. (See glossary for the houses in the appendix.)

You will want to use a natal chart for yourself that clearly shows the degrees and the houses. For the preferred chart to use with this book, visit www.beatrex.com and look for the link to download a free chart. You will need to know the date, time, and place of your birth.

Cosmic Check-In

"I" statements are designed specifically to keep you in touch with all of the signs and their houses each time the Moon is new or full. Fill in the blanks to complete each statement during each full and new moon phase to activate all parts of your birth chart and keep you in touch with Oneness. Have fun noticing how different you are during each cycle.

Blank Pages

Between each moon phase blank pages are provided for journaling.

Appendices

This section in the back of the book contains expanded information to support you as you work through the book; lists of the eclipses and retrogrades this year, and Tibetan Numerology, houses, heavenly bodies, Astro signs, colors, and Tarot glossaries.

January

We begin the second year of the transformational decade with Uranus, the ruler of our future, retrograde until the 13th of the month. This gives us chance to reset ourselves from the unifying factor of the year 2020 and set a new course of action in 2021, called "The Year of Adaptability." The power of Mars' action, along with Uranus' future focus, brings a new speed factor to the docile, slow moving tempo of the earth. This speed will assist the earth in the healing that is necessary for the required transformation.

January 1st-March 7th 2021 Jupiter and Saturn in Aquarius are coupled

It's time for the simplification and acceleration of our social lives, principles, associations, group involvement, contributions, and community. This will infuse the idea that humanity must rise up now!

January 6th Mars enters Taurus

This is a time for a change of values to come into play.

January 6th-31st Mars and Uranus coupled in Taurus

Acceleration of values happens here when action meets with innovation. The warrior and the rebel take on a cause to make the world a better place.

January 8th Mercury enters Aquarius

Be open to an advancement in the thinking department.

January 8th Venus enters Capricorn

It is time to be practical. Shopping is off the list for now. Time to find a new grounded way to value yourself. Impulsive action won't work.

January 14th Uranus goes direct in Taurus

Time to take on a new project that promotes your value.

January 20th The Sun enters Aquarius

Your mind will move from 'I think' to 'I know!'

January 28th Pluto is coupled with Venus

Expect some serious sensuality. Take the dive into deep intimacy.

January 28th Saturn, Sun, Jupiter tripled in Aquarius

I would expect a major directive from the Sun to get you to take part in a group or community that is making the way for a better place on earth. Get involved in a group of like-minded people and get the job done!

January 30th Mercury goes retrograde in Aquarius

Ask before you speak, "Is it kind?", "Is it truthful?", "Is it necessary?". Time to speak from our highest thought.

Super Sensitivity January 6th-8th and 10th-11th

Worry could take you down the rabbit hole. Remember, worry is the misuse of imagination.

Low Vitality January 24th and 25th

Expect to feel tired, the Earth is at a low right now, leaving you feeling exhausted. Self-care for the body is in the front row. Take the time out to do so.

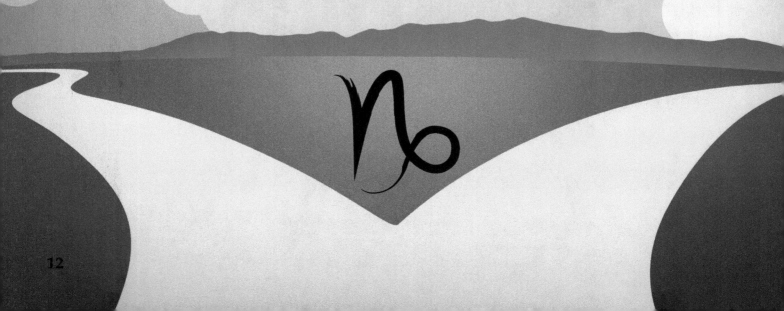

SUNDAY	MONDAY	TUESDAY	WEDNESDAY	THURSDAY	FRIDAY	SATURDAY
					1 ♅℞ Happy New Year 7. Start the year with a bigger picture.	2 ♅℞ ☽ V/C 1:59 PM ☽→♍ 5:13 PM 8. See any change as prosperity in action.
3 ♅℞ 9. Humanity needs your wisdom.	4 ♅℞ ☽ V/C 1:33 PM ☽→♎ 9:42 PM 10. Transformation involves a target.	5 ♅℞ 11. Universal knowledge is free.	6 ♅℞ ▲ ♂→♉ 2:26 PM ☽ V/C 9:54 PM 3. Play, dance, see the joy today.	7 ♅℞ ▲ ☽→♏ 12:53 AM 4. Start with the logical choice.	8 ♅℞ ▲ ☿→♒ 3:59 AM ♀→♑ 7:40 AM ☽ V/C 5:58 PM 5. Check options, new ideas will appear.	9 ♅℞ ☽→♐ 3:16 AM 6.What movement is best for your body?
10 ♅℞ ▲ ☽ V/C 10:29 AM 7. You are a wealth of knowledge.	11 ♅℞ ▲ ☽→♑ 5:30 AM 8. Your knowledge brings you wealth.	12 ♅℞ ● 23° ♑ 13' 9:01 PM ☽ V/C 11:21 PM 9. Be of loving service.	13 ♅℞ ☽→♒ 8:43 AM 10. Update your goals today.	14 ♅SD 6° ♉ 43' 12:36 AM ☽ V/C 1:27 AM 11. Trust what you know.	15 ☽→♓ 2:17 PM 3. Imagination has value, use it well.	16 4. Be the stability that is necessary.
17 ☽ V/C 7:44 PM ☽→♈ 11:08 PM 5. Keep things moving forward.	18 Martin Luther King 6. Loving service supports healing.	19 7. Quiet the mind to hear the answer.	20 ☽ V/C 12:28 AM ☽→♉ 10:56 AM ☉→♒ 12:39 PM 8. It's a big money day, go shopping!	21 9. A day for prayerful contemplation.	22 ☽ V/C 1:27 PM ☽→♊ 11:43 PM 10. Visualize the goal to completion.	23 11. Be open to a spiritual awakening.
24 ▼ ☽ V/C 11:17 PM 3. Put on your favorite music and dance.	25 ▼ ☽→♋ 10:51 AM 4. Having a plan makes the job easier.	26 5. Change doesn't wait, do it now.	27 ☽ V/C 9:54 AM ☽→♌ 6:55 PM 6. Bring beauty into your home.	28 ○ 9° ♌ 06' 11:16 AM 7. You do have an answer for a friend.	29 ☽ V/C 5:53 PM 8. Attend to your gratitude list.	30 ☿℞ ☽→♍ 12:03 AM ☿℞ 26° ♒ 29' 7:52 AM 9. Spirit listens.
31 ☿℞ 10. Be the visionary for someone.						

♈ Aries	♍ Virgo	♒ Aquarius	♀ Venus	♆ Neptune	V/C Void-of-Course	2. Balance	7. Learning
♉ Taurus	♎ Libra	♓ Pisces	♂ Mars	♇ Pluto	℞ Retrograde	3. Fun	8. Money
♊ Gemini	♏ Scorpio	☉ Sun	♃ Jupiter	→ Enters	SD Stationary Direct	4. Structure	9. Spirituality
♋ Cancer	♐ Sagittarius	☽ Moon	♄ Saturn	● New Moon	▲ Super Sensitivity	5. Action	10. Visionary
♌ Leo	♑ Capricorn	☿ Mercury	♅ Uranus	○ Full Moon	▼ Low Vitality	6. Love	11. Completion

New Moon in Capricorn

January 12th, 9:01 PM

When the Sun is in Capricorn

The statement for the Capricorn is I Use/I Produce. It is important for all of us to feel useful and productive during this time. When the Sun is in this sign, we are given opportunities to receive the blessings of abundance and prosperity on a concrete level. Material satisfaction is at the top of the priority list for Capricorn. This is why they are known to be ambitious. Let integrity and goodwill set the standard for your recognition and accomplishments. Now is the time to take advantage of the energy by being useful and productive with a higher purpose. The last few years Capricorn has been influenced by some major planets that have tested the character of the sign. Pluto is asking for transformation as it pushes towards a new definition of success and status. Saturn the ruler of Capricorn has been stationed there for a few years is asking for a new way to express tradition while moving beyond the bounds of perceived perfection.

Capricorn Goddess

Old Mother Frost whispers to you through the eons. The Spinner of Destiny and the Weaver of Fate, appears in many folktales with Neolithic roots in the earth goddesses of the seasons. A crone with names like Frau Holde or Mother Holle, she was an old woman who favored Capricorn traits like discipline and dedication and was said to punish those who shirked their duties. Grounding power draws you inward and inside, for cups of cocoa by the firelight, sleep and dreamtime. As you dream, you are not idle. You are busy gestating the visions of your renewal and building resilience through rest. 2020 brought gigantic changes and many-leveled disruptions that author Bruce Feiler called "life quakes." We are just now realizing the extent of their impacts. Now we lay the groundwork for recovery. Pull a tarot card for each month of 2021 to see what your new year holds. Allow yourself time to ponder, rest and rejuvenate; for it will provide the energy and space to create.

Build Your Altar

Colors	Forest green, tan, earth tones, deep red
Numerology	9 – Be of loving service
Tarot Card	The Devil – Confinement, attachment to form, look at the broader view
Gemstones	Topaz, carnelian, amber, smoky quartz, jasper
Plant Remedy	Rosemary – The power of memory
Fragrance	Frankincense – Opens the gateway for the Soul to enter the body

Moon Notes

New Moon 23° Capricorn 13'
New Moons are about opening new pathways for prosperity.

Element
Earth – Practical, determined, structured, enduring, stubborn, traditional, stable, and stuck inside the box.

Statement I Produce

Body Knees

Mind Ambition

Spirit Achievement

5th House Moon I Love/I Produce

Umbrella Energy
The way you love and how you want to be loved.

Choice Points
Action   Discussion
Non-action   Disinformation

Sabian Symbol
A Soldier Receiving Two Awards For Bravery In Combat.

Potential
Progress and empowerment.

Capricorn Victories & Challenges

Say all of the statements in this section out loud. Then, underline the phrase that means the most to you. Use the phrase as your affirmation for manifesting throughout this moon phase.

Ultimate fulfillment is mine today! My willingness to live my life to the fullest, each day, is making all of my dreams come true. I am fulfilling the promise of my destiny, and, in so doing, I make my mark on the world. I have completed my commitment to the Earth and to the cosmos by being all that I can be in the cycles of time on the inner and outer planes of awareness. All four seasons have been activated within me, so that I am in alignment and in motion with the cycles of releasing, rebirthing, planting, and harvesting. I can now claim my citizenship in all four worlds. I am open and ready for the inspiration that the spirit world brings me. I am ready to conquer the mental world by using thought, rather than thinking. I am open to the expression of my heart and the magnetic field of love that is ever-present in my experience. I am open to receive abundance from Nature and I contribute to the physical world by actively manifesting my ideas into reality. I am in harmony with the four elements and keep them active within me, as well as contribute to them externally. The element of air is within me as I breathe in the miracle of life. The element of earth is within me as I honor my body and use all of its senses to enhance the quality of life. I honor the Earth as my home and take complete stewardship of my home and property on this Earth. I honor the water, the wellspring of life eternal, and allow for the flow of my feelings and emotions to be a creative influence on the unconscious and conscious planes. I honor the fire within me as the spark of light that is a source of inspiration in my experience, and, in so doing, I have fulfilled the promise of my destiny to live fully, freely, and passionately on all levels and on all dimensions with my Earth-Cosmos connection.

Capricorn Homework

The Capricorn moon is the reincarnation of Spirit, emerging from the dark waters of our past emotions and releasing us from our fears of change and loss. Awaken your powerful and positive spiritual connection to be open to new possibilities. Ask yourself to move beyond your emotional loyalty to the past in order to manifest. We are reminded of our need for material and emotional security at this time. In order to insure this, we must learn to build a foundation for ourselves that is lit from within, and made from the materials of love, goodwill, and intelligence. Give yourself permission to throw away your watch and celebrate living in the moment.

Victory List

Acknowledge what you have overcome. Keep this list active during this moon cycle. Honoring victory allows you to accept success.

Tarot

Ask the question out loud, then draw a card. You may wish to draw it or paste a copy of it here. Then write down what you feel it might be telling you, in response to the question. Use the glossary in the appendix and record here anything about the card that captures your attention. You may wish to come back throughout the moon cycle to meditate or journal more on the card.

How is my body supporting my manifesting?

Manifesting List

This or something better than this comes to me in an easy and pleasurable way, for the good of all concerned. Thank you, Universe!

Capricorn Manifesting Ideas

Now is the time to focus on manifesting flexibility, productivity, authenticity, timing, new paradigms, transmuting, transformation, and re-translating structure.

New Moon in Capricorn

Your Personal Moon Experience

Fill in the Cosmic Check-In page. Then look up the Moon in the chart below. Take note of the "I" statement on the outside of the wheel where the Moon is located. This is the house the Moon is in, and the statement gives you the atmospheric energy, or the "umbrella energy" of this moon phase. This becomes the first statement to use in your mantra. Then, the "I" statement that corresponds with the astrological sign the Moon is in becomes the second statement (see *Moon Notes* for this moon phase). Now, locate the same sign and degree in your personal Natal chart and make a note of the house this degree falls in. The statement that corresponds with this house becomes your third statement. Go back to the Cosmic Check-In page and circle the three statements from the charts and read what you wrote. This will give you an idea about what to expect from this moon phase on a personal level. There is a video class that shows you how to read your personal chart at www.BlueMoonAcademy.com, look for *How to Use the Moon Book*.

I Love, I Produce, I _____ .

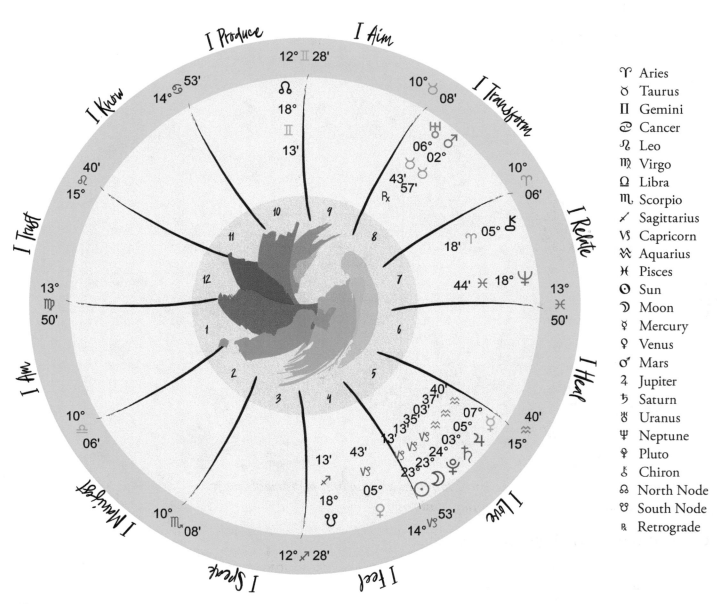

♈	Aries
♉	Taurus
♊	Gemini
♋	Cancer
♌	Leo
♍	Virgo
♎	Libra
♏	Scorpio
♐	Sagittarius
♑	Capricorn
♒	Aquarius
♓	Pisces
☉	Sun
☽	Moon
☿	Mercury
♀	Venus
♂	Mars
♃	Jupiter
♄	Saturn
♅	Uranus
♆	Neptune
♇	Pluto
⚷	Chiron
☊	North Node
☋	South Node
℞	Retrograde

Cosmic Check-In

Capricorn New Moon
January 12th, 9:01 PM

Take a moment to write a brief phrase for each "I" statement. This activates all areas of your life for this creative cycle.

♑ I Produce

♒ I Know

♓ I Trust

♈ I Am

♉ I Manifest

♊ I Speak

♋ I Feel

♌ I Love

♍ I Heal

♎ I Relate

♏ I Transform

♐ I Aim

Full Moon in Leo

January 28th, 11:16 AM

When the Sun is Opposite the Moon

Full moons are always in opposition to the Sun. This creates a feeling of tension between where you want to shine and how your feelings are flowing on a sensory level about the Sun's directive. The two forces seem like they are working against each other, yet they are on the same team displaying different techniques to obtain the same mission. The Leo/Aquarius polarity creates tension about the need to be adored and the need to be free.

Leo Goddess

Isis, Goddess of regeneration and rebirth, is a moon deity whose name means "throne." Most often pictured with a solar disk set atop horns, she governs the precise operation of the sun, moon and stars to guarantee the fertility of the earth. With radiant energy Isis is a sustainer who carries the ankh, a symbol of eternal life. She was worshiped throughout the Mediterranean world, as Iset or Aset in Egypt and Isis in Greece. With power, courage, pride and confidence, she triumphs over death and represents survival through intelligence, against all odds. Where does the fire of inspiration of Isis touch your soul? Light a candle and start up a conversation. Ask for her power and confidence as you navigate your 'new normal'. In the past year of pandemic fears, protests, economic uncertainty, and election chicanery, your DNA has been activated. Long embedded memories of past pandemics, fear, death and loss have been awakened. But also remember that imprinted in your DNA, are the memories of all your ancestors who survived. Isis calls to your body-memories of recovery, resilience, and healing. Allow the extraordinary break with 'normal' to be the crack that opens the way to an entirely new way of being. Isis lends her support, for the courage to fight, to change, to adapt, to shine. She brings victory over death, regeneration, lion's strength, and the light that sustains and renews.

Build Your Altar

Colors   Royal purple, gold, orange
Numerology   7 – You do have an answer for a friend
Tarot Card   The Sun – Follow the light, it knows where to go
Gemstones   Amber, emerald, pyrite, citrine, yellow topaz
Plant Remedy Sunflower – Standing tall in the center of life
Fragrance   Jasmine – Remembering your Soul's
                  original intention

Moon Notes

Full Moon   9° Leo 06'
Full Moons are about moving beyond blocks and setting yourself free.

Element
Fire – Igniting, dissolving, accelerating, cleansing, advancing awareness, impatience, leadership, passion, and vitality.

Statement   I Love

Body   Heart and Spine

Mind   Romance

Spirit   Generosity

4th House Moon   I Feel/I Love

Umbrella Energy
The way your early environmental training was and how that set your foundation for living, and why you chose your mother.

Karmic Awakening   Fantasy/Reality

Choice Points
Action   Enthusiasm
Non-action   Spin the Truth

Sabian Symbol
Early Morning Dew Sparkles As Sunlight Floods The Field.

Potential
New feelings merge with the light creating new space.

Clearing the Slate

Sixty hours before the full moon negative traits connected to the astro-sign might become activated to trigger what needs to be released during the full moon phase. You may notice wanting an unusual amount of attention, resistance to authority, or strong impatience that expresses itself as a brat attack. Make a list, look in the mirror, and for each negative trait, tell yourself *I am sorry, I forgive you, thank you for your awareness,* and *I love you.* Now is the time to start doing your Sky Power Yoga poses so your physiology can feel supported during this moon phase. The poses and the teaching are available on BlueMoonAcademy.com. Enjoy!

Leo Victories & Challenges

Say all of the statements in this section out loud. Then, underline the phrase that means the most to you. Use the phrase as your affirmation for releasing throughout this moon phase.

I no longer feel the need to be in control and dominated by my mind telling me that it is appropriate to repress my feelings. I am going to claim my dominion today and feel the power of life running through me. I accept the privilege of being fully human and fully alive. I look to see where I lack courage to connect to what is natural for me. I see where I have been stubborn and turn to face my resistance. I become aware of when my higher self says "Go" and my lower self says "No." I am aware that my lower self (my body) is a creature of habit and will sabotage me with the idea that change takes too much energy. I take responsibility for the part of me that is a creature of habit and talk to my body about coming into alignment with my new intention to become fully passionate and fully alive. I remember today that in order to get the body to move forward with me, I need two-thirds of my cells to align with my request. First, I become aware of the part of myself that is trying to control all of my outcomes and keep me a slave to those outcomes, rather than trusting in the evolution of nature and the concept of Divine Order. I give up the fight today knowing that this struggle is dissipating all my energy and making me exhausted. In order for my body to respond, I need to awaken my cells through sound and touch. So, today I rub my body and speak out loud by sharing my request for connection, revitalization, rejuvenation, passion, and support. Today, I celebrate the idea that I can connect to my wholeness by activating my cells to support my commitment to my aliveness. I can now stand tall in the center of life and grow in self-confidence.

Leo Homework

Review your memorabilia and see what no longer matches your current love nature, your creative nature, and your loving self. Set your heart free while chanting, "Love is all you need." Become a part of the new consciousness on the Earth that brings a more abundant life when we expand the radius of our love. Live Love Every Day!

Gratitude List

Keep this list active throughout the moon cycle. This will bring you to a level of completion so that a new cycle of opportunity can occur in your life. Be prepared for miracles!

Tarot

Ask the question out loud, then draw a card. You may wish to draw it or paste a copy of it here. Then write down what you feel it might be telling you, in response to the question. Use the glossary in the appendix and record here anything about the card that captures your attention. You may wish to come back throughout the moon cycle to meditate or journal more on the card.

How is my spirit supporting my releasing?

Releasing List

Say this statement out loud three times before writing your list:

I am a free spiritual being and it is my desire to be free to think and to express myself fully.

From this day forward I resolve to be true — first to myself and my highest self, and then to the highest self in me which is the Source of Love That I Am.

Leo Freedom Ideas

Now is the time to activate a game change in my life, and give up the need to be the center of attention, obstacles to generosity, false pride, false identity, blocks to confidence or creativity, excuses that keep me from quality time with my children, blocks to knowing that I am loved and lovable, and the idea that everyone needs to be devoted to me in all situations.

Full Moon in Leo

Your Personal Moon Experience

Fill in the Cosmic Check-In page. Then look up the Moon in the chart below. Take note of the "I" statement on the outside of the wheel where the Moon is located. This is the house the Moon is in, and the statement gives you the atmospheric energy, or the "umbrella energy" of this moon phase. This becomes the first statement to use in your mantra. Then, the "I" statement that corresponds with the astrological sign the Moon is in becomes the second statement (see *Moon Notes* for this moon phase). Now, locate the same sign and degree in your personal Natal chart and make a note of the house this degree falls in. The statement that corresponds with this house becomes your third statement. Go back to the Cosmic Check-In page and circle the three statements from the charts and read what you wrote. This will give you an idea about what to expect from this moon phase on a personal level. There is a video class that shows you how to read your personal chart at www.BlueMoonAcademy.com, look for *How to Use the Moon Book*.

I Feel, I Love, I _____.

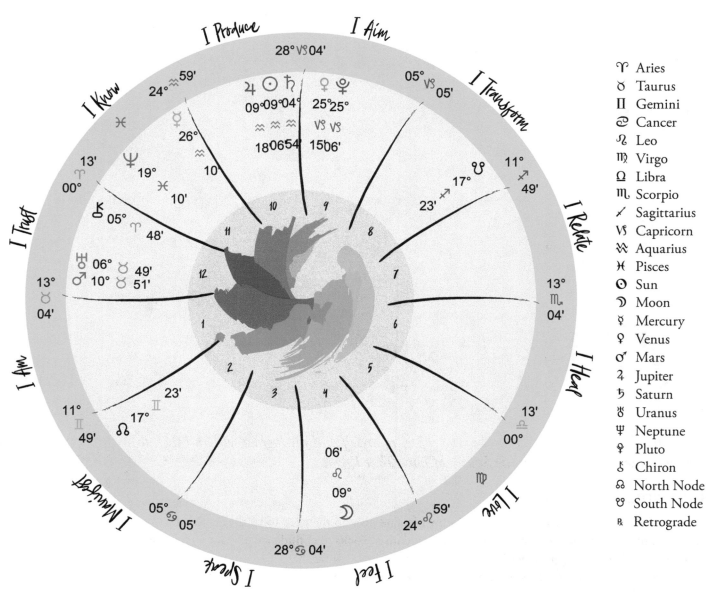

♈	Aries
♉	Taurus
♊	Gemini
♋	Cancer
♌	Leo
♍	Virgo
♎	Libra
♏	Scorpio
♐	Sagittarius
♑	Capricorn
♒	Aquarius
♓	Pisces
☉	Sun
☽	Moon
☿	Mercury
♀	Venus
♂	Mars
♃	Jupiter
♄	Saturn
♅	Uranus
♆	Neptune
♇	Pluto
⚷	Chiron
☊	North Node
☋	South Node
℞	Retrograde

Cosmic Check-In

Leo Full Moon
January 28th, 11:16 AM

Take a moment to write a brief phrase for each "I" statement. This activates all areas of your life for this creative cycle.

♌ I Love

♍ I Heal

♎ I Relate

♏ I Transform

♐ I Aim

♑ I Produce

♒ I Know

♓ I Trust

♈ I Am

♉ I Manifest

♊ I Speak

♋ I Feel

February

February 1st Mercury is retrograde in Aquarius until the 20th

Learn from your miscommunications. Ask what you have to do to reconcile with words so you can feel better about yourself.

February 1st Venus enters Aquarius

Expect an unusual urge to take on a different kind of love partner or experience. You may find yourself waking up with a stranger.

February 2nd Sun and Mercury retrograde conjunct in Capricorn

Time to take a long look at what you judge and work with the Law of Reflection. Ask yourself when judgment comes... "Am I judging what I am, what I fear, or what I lack?"

February 11th-16th Venus and Jupiter coupled in Aquarius

Expect many blessings to come forward in your personal life as well as your professional life and community life! Accept it, allow it, so BE it!

February 12th Lunar New Year

Enter the Ox. Expect to be strong, reliable, fair, conscientious, and inspire confidence in others as well as yourself. Trust is part of the good fortune for the year. You may feel very opinionated at times when choosing an unknown direction. The Ox energy will reward hardworking and methodical action.

February 18th The Sun enters Pisces

Expect a sensitive point of view to take over. Time for your creative process to promote a very positive outcome. Watch out for daydreaming. You could get lost.

February 25th Venus enters Pisces

Romance is flowing in like high tide heading for land. Allow yourself to experience the feelings in motion.

February 27th Jupiter, Mercury, and Saturn are dancing in Aquarius

This is a wonderful time to celebrate the acceleration of consciousness, a true trifecta on communicating blessings, and feeling the power of knowing!

Super Sensitivity February 7th-8th

Do your best to stay away from over-thinking, it could lead to anxiety or extra stress. Take a break for a few days so chaos doesn't make life difficult.

Low Vitality February 21st-22nd

Time for self-care. Pushing the envelope right now could lead to regret. The body comes first right now!

SUNDAY	MONDAY	TUESDAY	WEDNESDAY	THURSDAY	FRIDAY	SATURDAY

1 ☿℞
☽ V/C 3:09 AM
☽→♎ 3:25 AM
♀→♒ 6:05 AM
11. See what needs to be completed.

2 ☿℞
☽ V/C 10:15 PM
3. Use creativity today.

3 ☿℞
☽→♏ 6:15 AM
4. Connect to Mother Earth.

4 ☿℞
5. Expect an unexpected twist.

5 ☿℞
☽ V/C 1:19 AM
☽→♐ 9:16 AM
6. Loving care heals many wounds.

6 ☿℞
☽ V/C 10:15 PM
7. Knowledge is power.

7 ☿℞▲
☽→♑ 12:52 PM
8. Think big, manifest big!

8 ☿℞▲
9. Humanity craves kindness, be kind.

9 ☿℞
☽ V/C 9:21 AM
☽→♒ 5:21 PM
10. Listen to a TED Talk today.

10 ☿℞
11. Divine intention is yours today.

11 ☿℞
☽ V/C 11:05 AM
● 23° ♒ 17' 11:06 AM
☽→♓ 11:24 PM
3. Compliment someone.

12 ☿℞
Lunar New Year Enter the Ox
4. How strong is your foundation?

13 ☿℞
☽ V/C 11:28 PM
5. Relax and enjoy the ride today.

14 ☿℞
Valentine's Day
☽→♈ 7:54 AM
6. Live love in a large way.

15 ☿℞
President's Day
7. Your smarts will be noticed.

16 ☿℞
☽ V/C 4:16 PM
☽→♉ 7:12 PM
8. Go for your desires, it's possible.

17 ☿℞
9. Be aware of where you can help.

18 ☿℞
☉→♓ 2:43 AM
☽ V/C 11:27 PM
10. Take it to the next level today.

19 ☿℞
☽→♊ 8:03 AM
11. Universal knowledge is always there.

20
☿ SD 11° ♒ 01' 4:52 PM
3. It's a magical day.

21 ▼
☽ V/C 10:39 AM
☽→♋ 7:53 PM
4. Create a plan today.

22 ▼
5. Curiosity opens a new path.

23
☽ V/C 8:53 PM
6. Live love every day.

24
☽→♌ 4:23 AM
7. Listen to the language of wisdom.

25
♀→♓ 5:11 AM
8. Leadership skills are activated today.

26
☽ V/C 3:31 AM
☽→♍ 9:08 AM
9. Where can you be in service?

27
○ 8° ♍ 57' 12:18 AM
10. Start a new creative project.

28
☽ V/C 7:57 AM
☽→♎ 11:17 AM
11. Accept that you are empowered.

♈ Aries · ♍ Virgo · ♒ Aquarius · ♀ Venus · ♆ Neptune · V/C Void-of-Course · 2. Balance · 7. Learning
♉ Taurus · ♎ Libra · ♓ Pisces · ♂ Mars · ♇ Pluto · ℞ Retrograde · 3. Fun · 8. Money
♊ Gemini · ♏ Scorpio · ☉ Sun · ♃ Jupiter · → Enters · SD Stationary Direct · 4. Structure · 9. Spirituality
♋ Cancer · ♐ Sagittarius · ☽ Moon · ♄ Saturn · ● New Moon · ▲ Super Sensitivity · 5. Action · 10. Visionary
♌ Leo · ♑ Capricorn · ☿ Mercury · ♅ Uranus · ○ Full Moon · ▼ Low Vitality · 6. Love · 11. Completion

31

New Moon in Aquarius

February 11th, 11:06 AM

When the Sun is in Aquarius

This is a time when the higher octave of the mind comes into play and one is given the power of vision. The Aquarian energies promote knowing by being a wellspring of knowledge. They expand the radius of contact by going beyond the known in areas of communication and cooperation. Now is the time to be initiated into greater awareness to serve the fields of human endeavors. Connect and combine magic with science and become a creative influence. When the sun is in Aquarius we must unify with our team players and collect innovative ideas to advance the world to a better place.

Aquarius Goddess

In the olden tale, Mesopotamian Goddess Inanna invites herself to her sister Ereshkigal's husband's funeral. As Inanna has been the cause of the brother-in-law's death, Ereshkigal is angry. But she knows Inanna will not be allowed to return to life above ground, so she beckons Inanna to descend through the seven gates of the underworld, under one condition: Inanna must surrender her power, one item at a time. Inanna pays a high price and enters the palace stripped entirely bare and is sentenced to die. Ereshkigal hangs Inanna's carcass on a meat hook to rot. Symbolically, Inanna's ritualized ego death in the underbelly of the earth, leaves her without options or aid. Today Ereshkigal, Inanna's shadow sister, lays bare your false sense of security and demands brutal self-honesty. Light a candle and call in protection from your guides and angels. Summon the courage to ask Inanna for help. 2020 was a descent for us all to the depths of loneliness and grief. Now, it is time to re-emerge, through the seven chakra gates. Starting at the root chakra, give something to Ereshkigal that no longer serves you. Allow Inanna to gift you something in return, as you ascend the chakras from root to crown, rebirthing your power as you re-emerge from darkness. Remember to thank all who have assisted you.

Build Your Altar

Colors   Violet, neon, crystalline rainbow tints

Numerology 3 – Compliment someone

Tarot Card The Star – Golden opportunities for the future

Gemstones   Aquamarine, blue topaz, peacock pearls

Plant Remedy Queen of the Night Cactus – Ability to see light in the dark

Fragrance   Myrrh – Healing the nervous system

Moon Notes

New Moon 23° Aquarius 17'
New Moons are about opening new pathways for prosperity.

Element
Air – The breath of life that allows the mind to achieve new insights and fresh perspectives, abstract dreaming, freedom from attachments, codes of intelligence, and academic applications.

Statement I Know

Body Ankles

Mind Genius

Spirit Innovation

10th House Moon I Produce/I Know

Umbrella Energy
Your approach to status, career, honor, and prestige, and why you chose your father.

Choice Points
Action   Inner Peace
Non-action   Dissatisfaction

Sabian Symbol
A Man, Having Overcome His Passions, Teaches Deep Wisdom In Terms Of His Experience.

Potential
Learn from your experience.

Aquarius Victories & Challenges

Say all of the statements in this section out loud. Then, underline the phrase that means the most to you. Use the phrase as your affirmation for manifesting throughout this moon phase.

Today, I chart my course for my new direction. My future is set on a new, fresh evolutionary course. I am guided by a higher source and trust in that guidance. I know my life has value and I am willing to contribute to the pool of consciousness by experiencing my life and living my life to the fullest view of possibility. Today, I know my possibilities are endless. My Spirit and my Soul are connected to Heaven and to Earth and this knowing brings me to the awareness that I can add to the higher qualities of life because I am connected to the whole. My being is far-reaching and immeasurable. I contribute to existence simply by knowing. All of the guideposts are connected for me today to see my way to a profound new future. My vision is clear and I can clearly set my sights on this new course. Golden opportunities come with this new vision and I trust in my guidance to bring me to this new level of manifesting power. I check in with my inner lights, each day, by meditating and asking for all seven of the energy centers in my body to come into alignment with the outer symbols of guidance. I do this by becoming still and breathing until I feel the stillness. Then, I place my hand on each center in my body, one center at a time, to be activated by light. Next, I ask out loud for each center in my body to let me know what its energetic contribution to the new direction is and how best to use the energy to move forward on my new course of action. I write down each statement and connect each statement to the guiding star in the sky. I am now linked up physically and spiritually and ready to navigate my total self towards my new evolutionary direction.

Aquarius Homework

Aquarians manifest a storehouse of information through innovative telecommunications, technology, social networking and media, and global communication. They are typically found in the fields of psychology, science fiction authoring or film-making, speech writing, and aerospace engineering.

Consider these three Aquarian gifts:

- Opportunity – Become a creative influence
- Enlightenment – When you become aware that you are light
- Brotherhood – Separation doesn't exist anymore

Where do you see these occurring in your life?

Victory List

Acknowledge what you have overcome. Keep this list active during this moon cycle. Honoring victory allows you to accept success.

Tarot

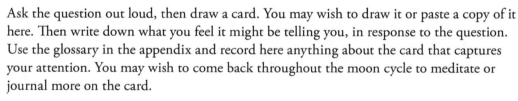

Ask the question out loud, then draw a card. You may wish to draw it or paste a copy of it here. Then write down what you feel it might be telling you, in response to the question. Use the glossary in the appendix and record here anything about the card that captures your attention. You may wish to come back throughout the moon cycle to meditate or journal more on the card.

How is my mind supporting my manifesting?

Manifesting List

This or something better than this comes to me in an easy and pleasurable way, for the good of all concerned. Thank you, Universe!

Aquarius Manifesting Ideas

Now is the time to focus on manifesting vision, invention, technology, freedom, friends, community, personal genius, higher awareness, teamwork, science, and magic.

New Moon in Aquarius

Your Personal Moon Experience

Fill in the Cosmic Check-In page. Then look up the Moon in the chart below. Take note of the "I" statement on the outside of the wheel where the Moon is located. This is the house the Moon is in, and the statement gives you the atmospheric energy, or the "umbrella energy" of this moon phase. This becomes the first statement to use in your mantra. Then, the "I" statement that corresponds with the astrological sign the Moon is in becomes the second statement (see *Moon Notes* for this moon phase). Now, locate the same sign and degree in your personal Natal chart and make a note of the house this degree falls in. The statement that corresponds with this house becomes your third statement. Go back to the Cosmic Check-In page and circle the three statements from the charts and read what you wrote. This will give you an idea about what to expect from this moon phase on a personal level. There is a video class that shows you how to read your personal chart at www.BlueMoonAcademy.com, look for *How to Use the Moon Book*.

I Produce, I Know, I _____ .

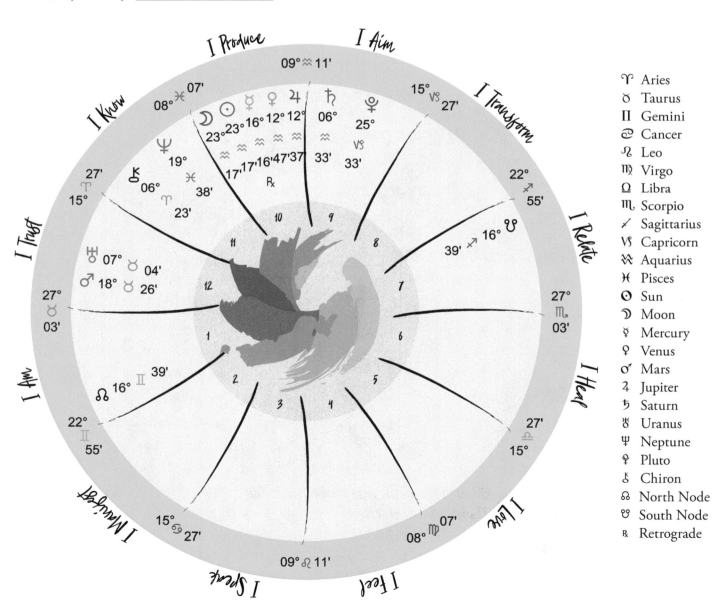

♈	Aries
♉	Taurus
♊	Gemini
♋	Cancer
♌	Leo
♍	Virgo
♎	Libra
♏	Scorpio
♐	Sagittarius
♑	Capricorn
♒	Aquarius
♓	Pisces
☉	Sun
☽	Moon
☿	Mercury
♀	Venus
♂	Mars
♃	Jupiter
♄	Saturn
♅	Uranus
♆	Neptune
♇	Pluto
⚷	Chiron
☊	North Node
☋	South Node
℞	Retrograde

Cosmic Check-In

Aquarius New Moon
February 11th, 11:06 AM

Take a moment to write a brief phrase for each "I" statement. This activates all areas of your life for this creative cycle.

♒ I Know

♓ I Trust

♈ I Am

♉ I Manifest

♊ I Speak

♋ I Feel

♌ I Love

♍ I Heal

♎ I Relate

♏ I Transform

♐ I Aim

♑ I Produce

Full Moon in Virgo

February 27th, 12:18 AM

When the Sun is Opposite the Moon

Full moons are always in opposition to the Sun. This creates a feeling of tension between where you want to shine and how your feelings are flowing on a sensory level about the Sun's directive. The two forces seem like they are working against each other, yet they are on the same team displaying different techniques to obtain the same mission. The Virgo/Pisces polarity creates tension between doing your work and finding your path.

Virgo Goddess

Astraea is the virgin Goddess of Purity who fled the earth upon seeing weaponry, warfare, and the rise of the patriarchy that destroyed the earth-goddess cultures during the Iron Age. She ascended to the heavens to become the constellation Virgo, to watch over the earth until she could one day return, on the day when humans were finally ready to usher in a new utopian age. Often depicted as a star maiden with wings and a shining halo or crown of stars, she carries a flaming torch or thunderbolt—the light of instantaneous truth and compassion.

If ever Astraea's healing is needed, it is now. She breathes in light and love, and showers us with a fresh new perspective, free from the restrictions of the past. Use your breath to release constriction from your heart space and locate the part of your physical body that is calling for healing love. With each long deep inhale, draw Astraea's purity, innocence, and sense of feminine grace into your body, wherever it is needed. As you breathe out, release grief from your lungs, along with heartache, loneliness, illness, worry, and anxiety wherever you may have stored them. As each person heals, that one will then reach out to heal the next, in a chain of love and light. Engage Astraea's blessings for your personal highest and best intentions, so the circle may expand for the healing of the earth.

Build Your Altar

Colors	Green, blue, earth tones
Numerology	10 – Start a new creative project
Tarot Card	The Hermit – Knowing your purpose and sharing it with the world
Gemstones	Emerald, sapphire
Plant remedy	Sage – The ability to hold and store light
Fragrance	Lavender – Management and storage of energy

Moon Notes

Full Moon 8° Virgo 57'
Full Moons are about moving beyond blocks and setting yourself free.

Element
Earth – Practical, determined, structured, enduring, stubborn, traditional, stable, and stuck inside the box.

Statement I Heal

Body Intestines

Mind Analytical

Spirit Divinity In the Details

9th House Moon I Aim/I Heal

Umbrella Energy
The way you approach spirituality, philosophy, journeys, higher knowledge, and aspiration.

Choice Points
Action   Mind Expansion
Non-action   Agitation

Sabian Symbol
An Expressionist Painter At Work.

Potential
Adding a creative expression to the day.

Clearing the Slate

Sixty hours before the full moon, negative traits connected to the astro-sign might become activated to trigger what needs to be released during the full moon phase. You may notice an extreme sense of judgement, an obsession for detail, or letting perfectionism stop your action. Make a list, look in the mirror, and for each negative trait, tell yourself *I am sorry, I forgive you, thank you for your awareness,* and *I love you.* Now is the time to start doing your Sky Power Yoga poses so your physiology can feel supported during this moon phase. The poses and the teaching are available on BlueMoonAcademy.com. Enjoy!

Virgo Victories & Challenges

Say all of the statements in this section out loud. Then, underline the phrase that means the most to you. Use the phrase as your affirmation for releasing throughout this moon phase.

Today I take time to go within to be silent. I imagine myself on a country road moving towards a beautiful mountain. I bask in the glory of the power of the mountain and know that it is calling me to the top. I find a pathway to the top and begin to climb. As I climb I become aware of a presence guiding me and empowering me to keep going, creating a sense of peacefulness within me.

I become aware of my own power in this silent journey to the top and revel in the serenity that nature and silence bring me. At last I am about to reach the summit and, just before I do, I feel the power drawing me to go within on a deeper level. I stop for a moment and look back at the path I have just climbed and know that my life's path is a remarkable gift. I connect to the center of the Earth and feel an inner glow.

The top of the mountain calls to me and, as I reach the top, a voice says to me, "Take in the view and look in all directions." As I turn 360-degrees, I sense a light igniting me in every direction. Then the voice says, "Look up!" Now, my awareness shifts and I see that I have become an illuminating light glowing in all six directions. Next I hear, "Sit in your silence and take in the vastness of who you are. Who you are is immeasurable." I sit, feeling the glow of light within me, and become aware of a greater plan for my life. I allow myself to receive this plan. I accept this assignment and slowly walk down the mountain, knowing that I can be a shining light for myself and others. I know I must take my light out to the world and share what I know to be my truth. Today, I become a messenger for the light.

Virgo Homework

Become integrated so that the light of your personality becomes soul-infused. When you are soul-infused and are in service to your Higher Self, you radiate love and light through the power of the inner self through all activities, thoughts, and emotions and become more magnificent. Learn the art of detachment and let your Soul take control.

Gratitude List

Keep this list active throughout the moon cycle. This will bring you to a level of completion so that a new cycle of opportunity can occur in your life. Be prepared for miracles!

Tarot

Ask the question out loud, then draw a card. You may wish to draw it or paste a copy of it here. Then write down what you feel it might be telling you, in response to the question. Use the glossary in the appendix and record here anything about the card that captures your attention. You may wish to come back throughout the moon cycle to meditate or journal more on the card.

How is my body supporting my releasing?

Releasing List

Say this statement out loud three times before writing your list:

I am a free spiritual being and it is my desire to be free to think and to express myself fully.

I hereby fully and completely free my mind from all adhesions to outdated philosophies, habits, relationships, groups of people, man-made laws, moral codes, all rules, set ideas and set ways of thinking, traditions, organizations, duty-motivated activities, guilt, judgment, and being misunderstood!

Virgo Freedom Ideas

Now is the time to activate a game change in my life, and give up finding fault with myself, my addiction to perfection, my addiction to detail, over-indulging in image management, pain-producing thinking patterns, judgment of others, resistance to being healthy, and destructive behaviors.

Full Moon in Virgo

Your Personal Moon Experience

Fill in the Cosmic Check-In page. Then look up the Moon in the chart below. Take note of the "I" statement on the outside of the wheel where the Moon is located. This is the house the Moon is in, and the statement gives you the atmospheric energy, or the "umbrella energy" of this moon phase. This becomes the first statement to use in your mantra. Then, the "I" statement that corresponds with the astrological sign the Moon is in becomes the second statement (see *Moon Notes* for this moon phase). Now, locate the same sign and degree in your personal Natal chart and make a note of the house this degree falls in. The statement that corresponds with this house becomes your third statement. Go back to the Cosmic Check-In page and circle the three statements from the charts and read what you wrote. This will give you an idea about what to expect from this moon phase on a personal level. There is a video class that shows you how to read your personal chart at www.BlueMoonAcademy.com, look for *How to Use the Moon Book*.

I Aim, I Heal, I _____ .

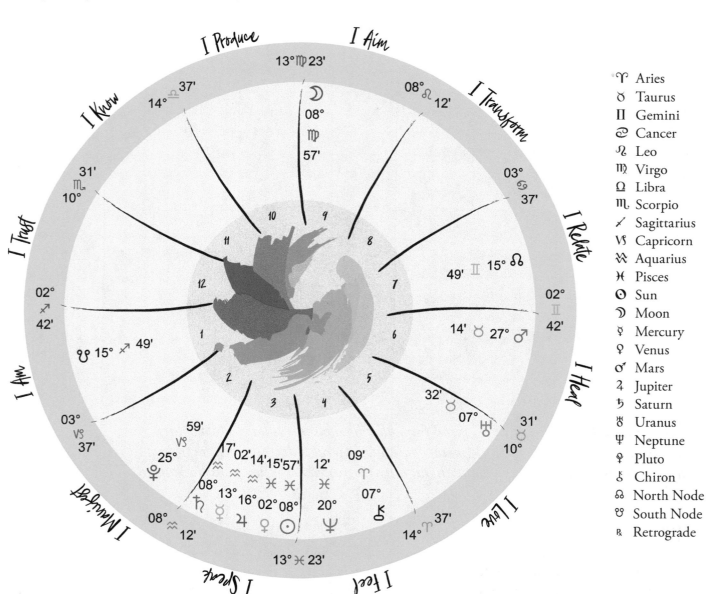

♈	Aries
♉	Taurus
♊	Gemini
♋	Cancer
♌	Leo
♍	Virgo
♎	Libra
♏	Scorpio
♐	Sagittarius
♑	Capricorn
♒	Aquarius
♓	Pisces
☉	Sun
☽	Moon
☿	Mercury
♀	Venus
♂	Mars
♃	Jupiter
♄	Saturn
♅	Uranus
♆	Neptune
♇	Pluto
⚷	Chiron
☊	North Node
☋	South Node
℞	Retrograde

Cosmic Check-In

Virgo Full Moon
February 27th, 12:18 AM

Take a moment to write a brief phrase for each "I" statement. This activates all areas of your life for this creative cycle.

♍ I Heal

♎ I Relate

♏ I Transform

♐ I Aim

♑ I Produce

♒ I Know

♓ I Trust

♈ I Am

♉ I Manifest

♊ I Speak

♋ I Feel

♌ I Love

March

March 3rd Mars enters Gemini and stays there all month

Expect a blast of energy that could lead to a deep yearning to travel. Take time to plan a major trip!

March 15th Mercury enters Pisces and stays there all month

Time to express your feelings to someone who is a good listener or make many new entries in your journal.

March 13th Venus conjunct Neptune in Pisces all month

A highly romantic time. This combo brings on a grand integration of conditional love with unconditional love. A super wave of creative influence could come flowing into your space. Take time to write down your feelings and ideas so they don't get lost. You may come in contact with an inspiration that can be life changing. A new pathway may appear that will bring you to a happy outcome.

March 20th The Sun enters Aries creating Spring Equinox

The Astrological New Year comes into being. The spark of light from Aries awakens all of life from the winter's sleep and gives space to a new manifested reality. It is now time to bring on your new reality. Go for it! Plant the seeds for your new dreams to come true!

March 21st Venus enters Aries

This is a 'wow' moment when impulsive action can move you far beyond your present reality if you allow it.

March 28th Mars conjunct North Node in Gemini and continues throughout the month

The North Node is a bold focus that directs you to your future. As it merges with Gemini it will bring about a need to communicate, broadcast, or write your ideas to bring them to the marketplace. Write a marketing plan, a book, a blog, or a newsletter. Broadcast your ideas on YouTube or start a podcast radio show!

March 29th Venus coupled with the Sun in Aries until 31st

On the personal side, impatience can become a reality and bring on brat attacks that you may regret later.

March 29th Mercury connected to Neptune in Pisces all month

Expect your senses to be at a heightened level of sensitivity. It may become a problem deciphering what is real and what is not real. Empathy could be difficult. Best to practice compassion so you can use your understanding without becoming toxic. Your incredible creativity and imagination can lead to a career in the arts such as painting, dance, or theatre, as well as healing or other fields of communication, where your ideas can touch and inspire others.

Super Sensitivity March 5th and 6th

Keep your feelings close to the vest on these days so they don't get caught up in the atmospheric chaos.

Low Vitality March 21st and 22nd

Earth changes could happen right now! Stay close to home and remember to say out-loud during these days, "I am in the right place at the right time for the most powerful experience!"

SUNDAY	MONDAY	TUESDAY	WEDNESDAY	THURSDAY	FRIDAY	SATURDAY
	1	**2** ☽ V/C 6:09 AM ☽→♏ 12:39 PM	**3** ♂→♊ 7:29 PM	**4** ☽ V/C 8:09 AM ☽→♐ 2:43 PM	**5▲**	**6▲** ☽ V/C 1:43 AM ☽→♑ 6:20 PM
	3. A playful, fun-loving day.	4. Planning serves you well today.	5. You may be asked to adapt and adjust.	6. Give a family member a call.	7. A good day to research a fun topic.	8. An 'ask and you shall receive' day.
7	**8** ☽ V/C 4:52 PM ☽→♒ 11:41 PM	**9**	**10** ☽ V/C 7:31 PM	**11** ☽→♓ 6:44 AM	**12**	**13** ● 23° ♓ 04' 2:22 AM ☽ V/C 8:37 AM ☽→♈ 3:44 PM
9. Nourish your soul by meditating.	10. What can you close the book on?	11. Take time to be thorough.	3. Get creative with a craft project.	4. A sound foundation makes it easy.	5. Answers appear during a walk.	6. Bring beauty into someone's day.
14 PDT begins 2:00 AM	**15** ♀→♓ 3:26 PM ☽ V/C 8:40 PM	**16** Mardi Gras ☽→♉ 3:57 AM	**17** Ash Wednesday St. Patrick's Day	**18** ☽ V/C 1:39 PM ☽→♊ 4:47 PM	**19**	**20** Spring Equinox ☉→♈ 2:37 AM
7. Join a discussion group or book club.	9. You are Divinely blessed.	10. Add a timeline to your goals.	11. Breathe in the power of All.	3. It's easy to be optimistic today.	4. Logic creates workable patterns.	5. Change it up and find freedom.
21▼ ☽ V/C 5:03 AM ☽→♋ 5:18 AM ♀→♈ 7:16 AM	**22▼**	**23** ☽ V/C 8:26 AM ☽→♌ 2:57 PM	**24**	**25** ☽ V/C 6:27 AM ☽→♍ 8:26 PM	**26**	**27** Passover Begins at Sunset ☽ V/C 4:47 PM ☽→♎ 10:23 PM
6. Check in with your neighbors.	7. How can you widen your mind?	8. Money grows in a variety of ways.	9. In stillness Spirit speaks.	10. The goal is attainable.	11. Acknowledge your limitlessness.	3. Have fun, party time!
28 Palm Sunday ○ 8° ♎ 18' 11:48 AM	**29** ☽ V/C 5:07 PM ☽→♏ 10:33 PM	**30**	**31** ☽ V/C 5:28 PM ☽→♐ 10:59 PM			
4. Teamwork makes work easier.	5. Empowerment brings new choices.	6. Love opens doors.	7. See a repeating lesson as learned.			

♈ Aries	♍ Virgo	♒ Aquarius	♀ Venus	♆ Neptune	V/C Void-of-Course	2. Balance
♉ Taurus	♎ Libra	♓ Pisces	♇ Pluto	℞ Retrograde	3. Fun
♊ Gemini	♏ Scorpio	☉ Sun	♂ Mars	→ Enters	⅜ Stationary Direct	4. Structure
♋ Cancer	♐ Sagittarius	☽ Moon	♄ Saturn	● New Moon	▲ Super Sensitivity	5. Action
♌ Leo	♑ Capricorn	☿ Mercury	♅ Uranus	○ Full Moon	▼ Low Vitality	6. Love

7. Learning
8. Money
9. Spirituality
10. Visionary
11. Completion

New Moon in Pisces

March 13th, 2:22 AM

When the Sun is in Pisces

This is a time when you come in contact with your most Divine essence. It is a time to meditate and connect to your higher purpose. Let your intuition guide you to a program of service. Let your Soul take control and connect to a space beyond your ego. In order to do this, you must become free of your habits, hang ups, and fantasies. Compassion frees you from the slavery of self-interest and the lure of your personality's blind urges, emotional traps, and mental crystallizations. When the Soul takes control, you unite your personality with Divine essence and radiate the light needed to find your true pathway.

Pisces Goddess

Yemaya, Mother of the Fishes, splashes into the water of our emotions at the cusp of a new year. Bringing yin/yang balance to energies, she cautions us to examine where we have been and where we are heading. Rising from ocean waters plagued by increasing temperatures, melting ice sheets, multiplying storm activity and pollution, she calls for a massive clearing. As the drum beats intensely, Yemaya swirls her wide ocean-blue skirt as she sways and moans. So much emotion, anger, disrespect. So much loss and grief. You feel her as she dances. Her movement calls for calm, for balance, for restoration. Clearing away the old to make way for the new, for all her children. With all you've been through, you too may feel the need to dance your sorrow, your anguish, your anger. You will need two pieces of music: one dark, undulating with repetitive beats, and sorrowful tones. Another light and flowing that brings your heart joy. Turn down the lights and turn up the volume. Tap into the depths of all that transpired in 2020 and allow Yemaya to flow through you as you dance. Put on the dark music and express your sorrow and let it all go. Cry if you need to. Break and journal your feelings. See if the release has brought some space. Then put on the light piece of music allowing your movement to express peace, healing, grace, and solace. Let joy live in your body. Journal again and share your experience.

Build Your Altar

Colors   Turquoise, blue, green, aqua

Numerology   6 – Bring beauty into someone's day

Tarot Card   The Moon – The inner journey, reflection, illumination

Gemstones   Amethyst, opal, jade, turquoise

Plant Remedy Passion flower – The ability to live in the here and now

Fragrance   Lotus – Connecting to the Divine without arrogance

Moon Notes

New Moon 23° Pisces 04'
New Moons are about opening new pathways for prosperity.

Element
Water – Taking the path of least resistance, going with the flow, secretive, sensual, glamorous, psychic, magnetic, escaping reality, a healer, an actor/actress, and creativity at its best.

Statement I Trust

Body Feet

Mind Service

Spirit Mystical

2nd House Moon I Manifest/I Trust

Umbrella Energy
The way you make your money and the way you spend your money.

Karmic Awakening I Am/We Are

Choice Points

Action   Sensitivity
Non-action   Sensationalism

Sabian Symbol
On A Small Island Surrounded By The Vast Expanse Of The Sea, People Are Seen Living In Close Interaction.

Potential
Give intimacy a chance.

Pisces Victories & Challenges

Say all of the statements in this section out loud. Then, underline the phrase that means the most to you. Use the phrase as your affirmation for manifesting throughout this moon phase.

I see my path clearly now. I know I must walk by myself on this journey into the deepest part of my Soul. It is time to clear the way and look beneath the surface to discover the parts of myself that I have placed in the unconscious world to be worked on at a later date. That later date is now. I am aware that the postponement of my inner reality can no longer be delayed.

Evolution is pulling me and it has become greater than my distractions, my fear, my denial, and my refusal to face what I have hidden from myself and others. I am aware of outside influences that pull me away from facing my inner realms. I know, without a doubt, that I am only as sick as the secrets I keep from myself and others. I see clearly how these distractions, illusions, and secrets need to be recognized so I can find the separated parts of myself that have been left in the dark, obscured from the light. I know that it is time to bring myself into wholeness and bring my shadow side to the light of my awareness.

I begin by closing my eyes and experiencing darkness. I imagine walking on a lonely road, in the dark, by myself. I pay particular attention to the sensations in my body and allow for the body to guide me to the places of dullness, numbness, fear, and anxiety. I simply allow for the intelligence of the body to coordinate the feeling with an image, person, or an event. I stay still and know, from the depth of my being, that recognition is all that is required of me right now. When recognition occurs, the light of awareness is ignited and the conscious world will take care of the rest. I know that the road to enlightenment requires me to first take the road into the dark side of my Soul.

Pisces Homework

Pisces manifest by using their psychic powers for counseling, therapy, hypnosis, the ministry, and creating spiritual schools or healing centers. They are also successful in visionary arts, acting, music, medical and pharmaceutical fields, and oceanography.

Take time to go within to discover where new pathways are open for advancement. Blessings pour forth to those who move toward these pathways in the spirit of service. Be open to these pathways and consider the ones that benefit our planet with new ideas, creative expression, and expanded views that lead people to higher levels of service.

Victory List

Acknowledge what you have overcome. Keep this list active during this moon cycle. Honoring victory allows you to accept success.

Tarot

Ask the question out loud, then draw a card. You may wish to draw it or paste a copy of it here. Then write down what you feel it might be telling you, in response to the question. Use the glossary in the appendix and record here anything about the card that captures your attention. You may wish to come back throughout the moon cycle to meditate or journal more on the card.

How is my heart supporting my manifesting?

Manifesting List

*This or something better than this comes to me in an easy and pleasurable way,
for the good of all concerned. Thank you, Universe!*

Pisces Manifesting Ideas

Now is the time to focus on manifesting connection with the Divine, creativity, healing
powers, psychic abilities, sensitivity, compassion, and service.

New Moon in Pisces

Your Personal Moon Experience

Fill in the Cosmic Check-In page. Then look up the Moon in the chart below. Take note of the "I" statement on the outside of the wheel where the Moon is located. This is the house the Moon is in, and the statement gives you the atmospheric energy, or the "umbrella energy" of this moon phase. This becomes the first statement to use in your mantra. Then, the "I" statement that corresponds with the astrological sign the Moon is in becomes the second statement (see *Moon Notes* for this moon phase). Now, locate the same sign and degree in your personal Natal chart and make a note of the house this degree falls in. The statement that corresponds with this house becomes your third statement. Go back to the Cosmic Check-In page and circle the three statements from the charts and read what you wrote. This will give you an idea about what to expect from this moon phase on a personal level. There is a video class that shows you how to read your personal chart at www.BlueMoonAcademy.com, look for *How to Use the Moon Book*.

I Manifest, I Trust, I _____ .

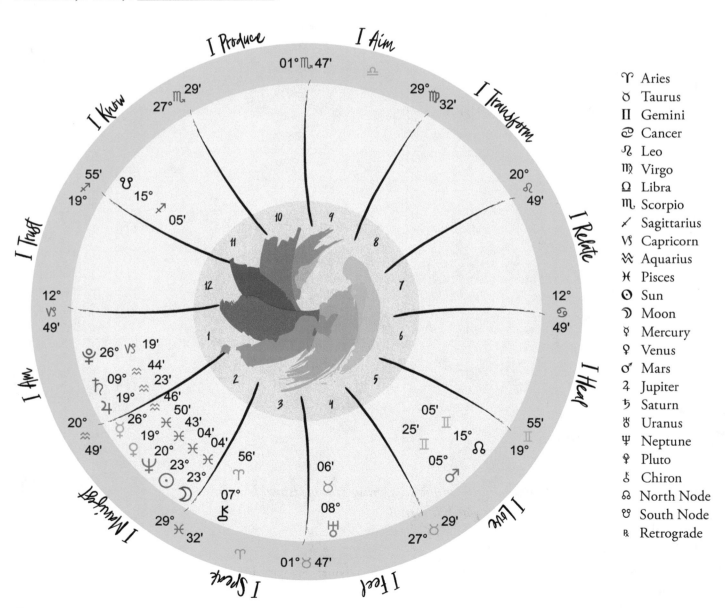

♈	Aries
♉	Taurus
♊	Gemini
♋	Cancer
♌	Leo
♍	Virgo
♎	Libra
♏	Scorpio
♐	Sagittarius
♑	Capricorn
♒	Aquarius
♓	Pisces
☉	Sun
☽	Moon
☿	Mercury
♀	Venus
♂	Mars
♃	Jupiter
♄	Saturn
♅	Uranus
♆	Neptune
♇	Pluto
⚷	Chiron
☊	North Node
☋	South Node
℞	Retrograde

Cosmic Check-In

Pisces New Moon
March 13th, 2:22 AM

Take a moment to write a brief phrase for each "I" statement. This activates all areas of your life for this creative cycle.

♓ I Trust

♈ I Am

♉ I Manifest

♊ I Speak

♋ I Feel

♌ I Love

♍ I Heal

♎ I Relate

♏ I Transform

♐ I Aim

♑ I Produce

♒ I Know

Full Moon in Libra

March 28th, 11:48 AM

When the Sun is Opposite the Moon

Full moons are always in opposition to the Sun. This creates a feeling of tension between where you want to shine and how your feelings are flowing on a sensory level about the Sun's directive. The two forces seem like they are working against each other, yet they are on the same team displaying different techniques to obtain the same mission. The Libra/Aries polarity creates tension between the idea of "We" versus "Me."

Libra Goddess

Themis, Goddess of Justice, brings balance and fairness into your awareness this moon. She is here to assist in building a new divine order, true to ideals for the benefit of all. Themis asks you to open your ears and listen, instead of speaking. Look from Themis's bird's-eye view to see possibilities for leaving the old ways behind. Your perspective may broaden and change as you take small steps outside of your comfort zone. Listen without formulating an opinion or argument to respond with. Take a walk in a neighborhood where your supposed "opponents" live. Be willing to see and hear another's reality. With a compassionate heart, feel their pain and hear their calls for justice. Then, with this new awareness, be witness to your own pain and articulate your own need for justice. You will learn there are no sides, no opponents, no black and white answers. Themis brings her good counsel along with ideas for pragmatic action and sincere negotiation.

Action, borne of the social protests of 2020, will begin to flower and bear fruit this spring. New laws, procedures, practices, and community input will require careful thought and planning, considering all that has been revealed and all that has been learned. Open your heart to listen and learn, accept and adapt. The scales of justice only balance when everyone's cup is full.

Build Your Altar

Colors	Pink, green
Numerology	4 – Teamwork makes work easier
Tarot Card	Justice – Positive and negative uses of karma
Gemstones	Rose quartz, jade
Plant remedy	Olive trees – Stamina
Fragrance	Eucalyptus – Clarity of breath

Moon Notes

Full Moon 8° Libra 18'
Full Moons are about moving beyond blocks and setting yourself free.

Element
Air – The breath of life that allows the mind to achieve new insights and fresh perspectives, abstract dreaming, freedom from attachments, codes of intelligence, and academic applications.

Statement I Relate

Body Kidneys

Mind Relationship

Spirit Peace

4th House Moon I Feel/I Relate

Umbrella Energy
The way your early environmental training was and how that set your foundation for living, and why you chose your mother.

Karmic Awakenings
My Money/Our Money

Choice Points
Action   Symmetry
Non-action   Severity

Sabian Symbol
Having Passed Through Narrow Rapids, A Canoe Reaches Calm Waters.

Potential
Life will get easier now!

Clearing the Slate

Sixty hours before the full moon negative traits connected to the astro-sign might become activated to trigger what needs to be released during the full moon phase. You may notice an unusual need to defend, an over-shadowing guilt, or a need to justify. Make a list, look in the mirror, and for each negative trait, tell yourself *I am sorry, I forgive you, thank you for your awareness,* and *I love you.* Now is the time to start doing your Sky Power Yoga poses so your physiology can feel supported during this moon phase. The poses and the teaching are available on BlueMoonAcademy.com.

Libra Victories & Challenges

Say all of the statements in this section out loud. Then, underline the phrase that means the most to you. Use the phrase as your affirmation for releasing throughout this moon phase.

I am awakened to the reality of the Law of Cause and Effect. I take time out today to see what is coming back to me. I know my actions, my words, and my thoughts have life and manifest in a pattern that returns to me. Today, I am in a place where I can clearly see the results of my words, my actions, and my thoughts. I am aware that it is time for a review and, in so doing, I am given the opportunity to balance, integrate and redistribute these results in a more productive way. When I truly know and experience the Law of Cause and Effect (what I send out comes back to me), I can take responsibility for my actions, words, and thoughts, and set myself free of blame. When blame is gone from my thought pattern (self-inflicted or circumstantial), I am able to benefit from my review rather than wasting energy justifying or defending my position. I now accept the idea that I am free to reconcile with whatever I have labeled as an injustice in my life. I take the time to re-route my thinking towards making life a beneficial experience. Today, I accept that in changing my language I can change my life. Today, I prepare to take actions toward beneficial experiences. Today, I release the need to be right and accept the right to be. Today, I stop judging life and start living life.

Libra Homework

Let the fresh air blow away mental stagnation related to times when you let others' interests supersede your own. Drink an excess amount of water to alert your kidneys that the recalibration process has commenced. It's time to deepen your intention to be one with the light, promoting restoration on Earth.

Gratitude List

Keep this list active throughout the moon cycle. This will bring you to a level of completion so that a new cycle of opportunity can occur in your life. Be prepared for miracles!

Tarot

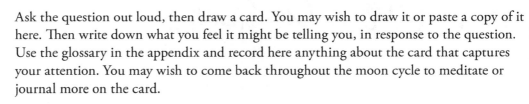

Ask the question out loud, then draw a card. You may wish to draw it or paste a copy of it here. Then write down what you feel it might be telling you, in response to the question. Use the glossary in the appendix and record here anything about the card that captures your attention. You may wish to come back throughout the moon cycle to meditate or journal more on the card.

How is my mind supporting my releasing?

Releasing List

Say this statement out loud three times before writing your list:

I am a free spiritual being and it is my desire to be free to think and to express myself fully.

I hereby fully and completely free my mind from all adhesions to outdated philosophies, habits, relationships, groups of people, man-made laws, moral codes, all rules, set ideas and set ways of thinking, traditions, organizations, duty-motivated activities, guilt, judgment, and being misunderstood!

Libra Freedom Ideas

Now is the time to activate a game change in my life, and give up situations that are not balanced, people-pleasing and the need to be liked, sorrow over past relationships, unsupportive relationships, the need to be right, false accusations, and being misunderstood.

Full Moon in Libra

Your Personal Moon Experience

Fill in the Cosmic Check-In page. Then look up the Moon in the chart below. Take note of the "I" statement on the outside of the wheel where the Moon is located. This is the house the Moon is in, and the statement gives you the atmospheric energy, or the "umbrella energy" of this moon phase. This becomes the first statement to use in your mantra. Then, the "I" statement that corresponds with the astrological sign the Moon is in becomes the second statement (see *Moon Notes* for this moon phase). Now, locate the same sign and degree in your personal Natal chart and make a note of the house this degree falls in. The statement that corresponds with this house becomes your third statement. Go back to the Cosmic Check-In page and circle the three statements from the charts and read what you wrote. This will give you an idea about what to expect from this moon phase on a personal level. There is a video class that shows you how to read your personal chart at www.BlueMoonAcademy.com, look for *How to Use the Moon Book*.

I Feel, I Relate, I _____.

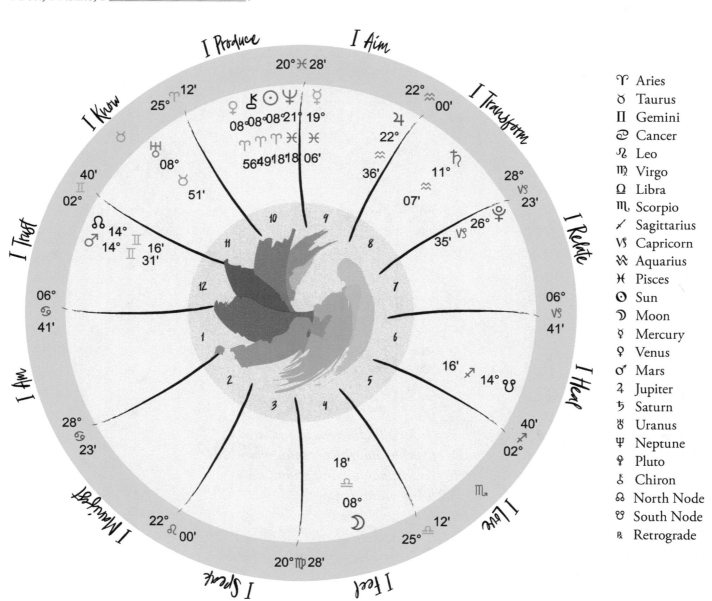

♈	Aries
♉	Taurus
♊	Gemini
♋	Cancer
♌	Leo
♍	Virgo
♎	Libra
♏	Scorpio
♐	Sagittarius
♑	Capricorn
♒	Aquarius
♓	Pisces
☉	Sun
☽	Moon
☿	Mercury
♀	Venus
♂	Mars
♃	Jupiter
♄	Saturn
♅	Uranus
♆	Neptune
♇	Pluto
⚷	Chiron
☊	North Node
☋	South Node
℞	Retrograde

Cosmic Check-In

Libra Full Moon
March 28th, 11:48 AM

Take a moment to write a brief phrase for each "I" statement. This activates all areas of your life for this creative cycle.

♎ I Relate

♏ I Transform

♐ I Aim

♑ I Produce

♒ I Know

♓ I Trust

♈ I Am

♉ I Manifest

♊ I Speak

♋ I Feel

♌ I Love

♍ I Heal

April

April 3rd Mercury enters Aries

There may be a tendency to talk too much about yourself. It's a good time to make decisions about the way you want to be recognized. A marketing plan, product introduction, and/or résumés can be easily written and have a favorable outcome.

April 11th Moon conjunct Venus

You may experience a huge need to be nurtured. Make time to connect with your mother. Hugging is a good idea right now!

April 11th Mercury coupled with the Sun

A great time to promote your project. Creating your marketing plan right now could bring you major success. Personal promo packets will work in your favor.

April 12th Mars still influences the North Node

This is creating a dynamic advancement to get you closer to your future destiny. As they say in Feng Shui, follow the chi. It will take you where you need to be to get the best out of your life.

April 14th Venus enters Taurus

This is a time to create your life filled with luxury, comfort, sensuality, and abundance. Keep your manifest list updated—the juicier the better!

April 19th Mercury enters Taurus

We will become less impulsive and indecisive with our thought processes. When Mercury is in Taurus, our thinking is down-to-earth, solid, and grounded.

April 19th The Sun moves into Taurus

This is a time to dive into your natural self and take a break. Surround yourself in luxury, beauty, and comfort. You may notice the urge to go shopping. Remember your job here is to add divinity to the material world. Thus, enhancing all that is around you.

April 23rd Mars enters Cancer

This could create action in and around the home. It may be time to redecorate or remodel or move to a new home. On a family level, it is time to arrange activities with relatives. You may feel like planning a family reunion or a trip to be with family.

April 26th The Sun, Uranus, Venus, and Mercury quadrupled in Taurus

This is an energetic time to bring new light and a ton of activity into your life. Expect urges to be free. Go shopping, go dancing, and expect to live the life of luxury.

April 27th Pluto goes retrograde

When Pluto goes retrograde, it is time to reset yourself in many areas that you may keep hidden from yourself and others. This is a time when light can enter the shadow side and bring forth many 'a-has' around money, sex, power, taxes and death. Reset, rewind and set yourself free. The theme is transformation. Accept it and know in so doing, blessings will abound.

Super Sensitivity April 1st-2nd and 29th-30th

You may experience an overly active confusion in the air. Remember this sensitivity is universal not personal. Do your best to keep it that way.

Low Vitality April 16th-17th and 20th-24th

On the 16th and 17th slow down and take time to smell the roses. Going too fast could be hazardous to your health. On the 20th through 24th, Mars enters the Low Vitality zone. This could lead to a hyperactive Earth and create earth changes. Take really good care of yourself at this time and set the intention that you will be in the right place at the right time! Stay close to home!

SUNDAY	MONDAY	TUESDAY	WEDNESDAY	THURSDAY	FRIDAY	SATURDAY
				1▲ April Fools' Day 8. Follow through and success is yours.	2▲ Good Friday ☽ V/C 10:23 PM 9. Every moment is a spiritual moment.	3 ☽→♑ 1:13 AM ☿→♈ 8:41 PM 10. Focus on the goal instead of what was.
4 **Easter** **Passover Ends at Nightfall** 11. We are one.	5 ☽ V/C 12:05 AM ☽→♒ 6:04 AM 3. Make a play date.	6 4. Sorry, it's a day to be practical.	7 ☽ V/C 3:04 AM ☽→♓ 1:30 PM 5. Say yes to a different thought or idea.	8 6. Give love, be love.	9 ☽ V/C 4:48 PM ☽→♈ 11:11 PM 7. Lessons learned become wisdom.	10 8. Leaders take risks and prosper.
11 ● 22° ♈ 25' 7:31 PM 9. Kindness works miracles.	12 **Ramadan Begins at Sunset** ☽ V/C 5:06 AM ☽→♉ 10:44 AM 10. Follow intention with attention.	13 11. Find inspiration today.	14 ☽ V/C 4:59 AM ♀→♉ 11:22 AM ☽→♊ 11:35 PM 3. Let your dreams become reality.	15 4. Let patience be your friend today.	16▼ 5. Be willing to accept change.	17▼ ☽ V/C 8:02 AM ☽→♋ 12:26 PM 6. Allow nature to nurture you.
18 7. Sign up for a new class today.	19 ☿→♉ 3:29 AM ☉→♉ 1:33 PM ☽ V/C 5:03 PM ☽→♌ 11:10 PM 8. Passion manifests prosperity.	20▼ 9. Pray for a friend.	21▼ 10. Turn your dreams into goals.	22▼ **Earth Day** ☽ V/C 5:04 AM ☽→♍ 6:08 AM 11. Awareness expands into grace.	23▼ ♂→♋ 4:49 AM 3. It's all fun and games today.	24▼ ☽ V/C 3:49 AM ☽→♎ 9:06 AM 4. How strong is your foundation?
25 5. Yes, it's okay to change your plan.	26 ☽ V/C 5:39 AM ☽→♏ 9:19 AM ○ 7° ♏ 06' 8:31 PM 6. Give your health your priority.	27♇℞ ♇℞ 26° ♑ 48' 1:02 PM 7. Use wisdom to be all that you are.	28♇℞ ☽ V/C 5:31 AM ☽→♐ 8:43 AM 8. Bring it on! You will succeed.	29♇℞▲ 9. Service is harmonizing for your soul.	30♇℞▲ ☽ V/C 6:26 AM ☽→♑ 9:16 AM 10. Take a look at new technology.	

♈ Aries	♍ Virgo	♒ Aquarius	♀ Venus	♆ Neptune	V/C Void-of-Course	2. Balance	7. Learning
♉ Taurus	♎ Libra	♓ Pisces	♂ Mars	♇ Pluto	℞ Retrograde	3. Fun	8. Money
♊ Gemini	♏ Scorpio	☉ Sun	♃ Jupiter	→ Enters	SD Stationary Direct	4. Structure	9. Spirituality
♋ Cancer	♐ Sagittarius	☽ Moon	♄ Saturn	● New Moon	▲ Super Sensitivity	5. Action	10. Visionary
♌ Leo	♑ Capricorn	☿ Mercury	♅ Uranus	○ Full Moon	▼ Low Vitality	6. Love	11. Completion

New Moon in Aries

April 11th, 7:31 PM

When the Sun is in Aries

Aries awakens the dreamer from Winter sleep and represents the raw energy of Spring, when the new shoots of life burst forth. Aries is the fundamental, straightforward approach to life. There is no challenge that is too great, no obstacle too daunting, and no rival too powerful for the Aries. Aries symbolizes initiation, leadership, strength, and potency. Competition and achievement are very important to Aries. Now is the time to be a pioneer and break all barriers to become the winner you are.

Aries Goddess

Brigid was a pre-Christian Sun Goddess of Ireland, who in later years was syncretized into the Christian church as Saint Brigid of Kildare. She was a goddess of dawn light and springtime renewal, whose name meant "exalted one." She was also the Goddess of the Well, of high places and low. Bonfires were lit in her honor. In Winged Destiny, Fiona MacLeod tells us of Brigid, "I put songs and music on the wind before ever the bells of the chapel were rung in the West or hearth in the East…And I have been a breath in your heart. And the day has its feet to it that will see me coming into the hearts of men and women like a flame upon dry grass, like a flame of wind in a great wood." Now is the time for the return of the feminine divine. Brigid asks you to celebrate your identity and inner light—your unique song. Look in the mirror, deep into your eyes, and say "You are the Goddess, your Light shines, your Love heals." As you do this imagine Brigid standing behind you with her hands on your shoulders. Say it until you mean it and you believe it. Then turn your brilliance into purposeful action.

Build Your Altar

Colors	Red, black, white
Numerology	9 – Kindness works miracles
Tarot Card	Emperor – Success on all levels
Gemstones	Diamond, red jasper, coral, obsidian
Plant Remedy	Pomegranates, oak – Planting new life, rooting new life
Fragrance	Ginger – The ability to ingest and digest life

Moon Notes

New Moon 22° Aries 25'
New Moons are about opening new pathways for prosperity.

Element
Fire – Igniting, dissolving, accelerating, cleansing, advancing awareness, impatience, leadership, passion, and vitality.

Statement I Am

Body Head

Mind Warrior

Spirit Winning/Leadership

6th House Moon I Heal/I Am

Umbrella Energy
The way you manage your body and its appearance.

Karmic Awakening Self Love/Group Love

Choice Points
Action   Anticipation
Non-action   Pessimism

Sabian Symbol
A Pregnant Woman In A Light Summer Dress.

Potential
Holding the space for new life.

Aries Victories & Challenges

Say all of the statements in this section out loud. Then, underline the phrase that means the most to you. Use the phrase as your affirmation for manifesting throughout this moon phase.

I am the author of my life. I accept that I am a winner and, in so doing, all doors are open to me. I hold the world in the palm of my hand and I know that there is not a mountain that I cannot climb. My ability to respond to life is in operation today and I direct my intention to bring me to the next level of self-determined achievement. The world and its systems are available for me to use as tools for my success and I use them with true excellence. I am organized and all systems are in place for me to make my mark on the world. I accept that my structured ground state and my dynamic energy are ready to make headway using pure determination, action, planning, and power. I will manage this plan and know that the sequence of events provided support me to make a breakthrough today.

I am willing to make my plan and take action on it. I gather my support team together today to focus on the appropriate action and encourage each person in their area of excellence and production. I am a great leader and my dynamic power is a good resource for others to determine their own success formula. I am aware that all parts of my team are important and place value on all areas of performance required to manifest in the world. I know how to place people in their best areas of expertise, so they can experience their own unique talent manifesting. Today, I honor my father for what he taught me by what he did, or didn't do, to encourage my ability to perform. I am the producer. I am the protector. I am the provider. I am the promoter. I am power. I am the author of my life.

Aries Homework

Aries manifest best through sales and promotions, and as a professional athlete, personal trainer or coach, martial arts expert, military professional, demolition expert, fireworks manufacturer, or wardrobe consultant.

Merge your light and dark forces so balance can occur. Then, give shape to your feelings through creative forms and learn to live in the duality of your Soul and watch your spirit soar! The embodiment of this duality connects you to the Unity, a requirement for these times.

Victory List

Acknowledge what you have overcome. Keep this list active during this moon cycle. Honoring victory allows you to accept success.

Tarot

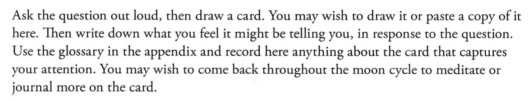

Ask the question out loud, then draw a card. You may wish to draw it or paste a copy of it here. Then write down what you feel it might be telling you, in response to the question. Use the glossary in the appendix and record here anything about the card that captures your attention. You may wish to come back throughout the moon cycle to meditate or journal more on the card.

How is my spirit supporting my manifesting?

Manifesting List

This or something better than this comes to me in an easy and pleasurable way, for the good of all concerned. Thank you, Universe!

Aries Manifesting Ideas

Now is the time to focus on manifesting personality power, leadership, strength, self-acceptance, winning, courage, personal appearance, and advancing to new frontiers.

New Moon in Aries

Your Personal Moon Experience

Fill in the Cosmic Check-In page. Then look up the Moon in the chart below. Take note of the "I" statement on the outside of the wheel where the Moon is located. This is the house the Moon is in, and the statement gives you the atmospheric energy, or the "umbrella energy" of this moon phase. This becomes the first statement to use in your mantra. Then, the "I" statement that corresponds with the astrological sign the Moon is in becomes the second statement (see *Moon Notes* for this moon phase). Now, locate the same sign and degree in your personal Natal chart and make a note of the house this degree falls in. The statement that corresponds with this house becomes your third statement. Go back to the Cosmic Check-In page and circle the three statements from the charts and read what you wrote. This will give you an idea about what to expect from this moon phase on a personal level. There is a video class that shows you how to read your personal chart at www.BlueMoonAcademy.com, look for *How to Use the Moon Book*.

I Heal, I Am, I _____ .

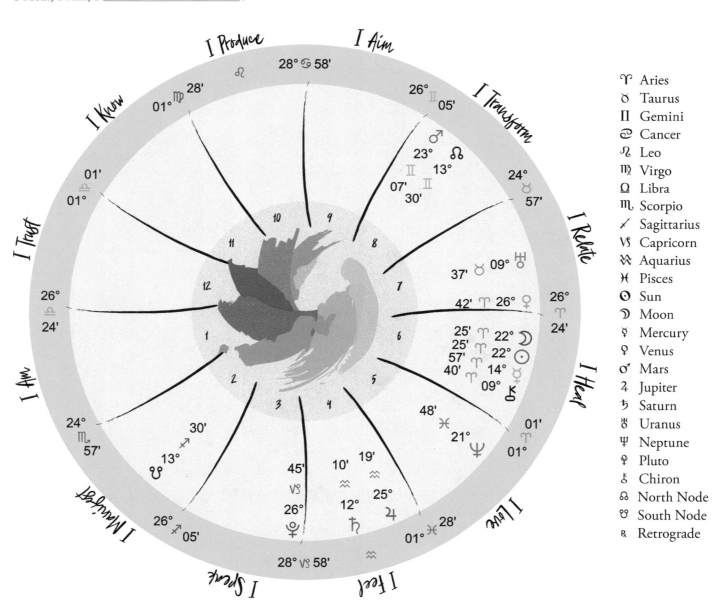

♈	Aries
♉	Taurus
♊	Gemini
♋	Cancer
♌	Leo
♍	Virgo
♎	Libra
♏	Scorpio
♐	Sagittarius
♑	Capricorn
♒	Aquarius
♓	Pisces
☉	Sun
☽	Moon
☿	Mercury
♀	Venus
♂	Mars
♃	Jupiter
♄	Saturn
♅	Uranus
♆	Neptune
♇	Pluto
⚷	Chiron
☊	North Node
☋	South Node
℞	Retrograde

Cosmic Check-In

Aries New Moon
April 11th, 7:31 PM

Take a moment to write a brief phrase for each "I" statement. This activates all areas of your life for this creative cycle.

♈ I Am

♉ I Manifest

♊ I Speak

♋ I Feel

♌ I Love

♍ I Heal

♎ I Relate

♏ I Transform

♐ I Aim

♑ I Produce

♒ I Know

♓ I Trust

Full Moon in Scorpio

April 26th, 8:31 PM

When the Sun is Opposite the Moon

Full moons are always in opposition to the Sun. This creates a feeling of tension between where you want to shine and how your feelings are flowing on a sensory level about the Sun's directive. The two forces seem like they are working against each other, yet they are on the same team displaying different techniques to obtain the same mission. The Scorpio/Taurus polarity creates tension between sharing resources and living abundantly for yourself.

Scorpio Goddess

Kali comes as your last resort. She appears when all else has failed, there are no clear answers, but a path must be forged. Bridges have been burned and you've no home to go back to. Change is no longer impossible, difficult or unthinkable, it is inevitable. You are fearless. Kali feeds your first and second chakras, survival at all costs and the creativity to birth a new reality. She manifests from the power of your emotions, your gut-level inner knowing, spiced with a dose of desperation, from the dark recesses of a wound begging to be healed. Our society has a vast emotional backlog of buried secrets, pain and injustices. Kali asks you to face it, tell all the stories, speak the pain and be completely heard before the transformation may occur. Start by feeling the deep-seeded anger, move through screaming and crying, railing at the system, and don't take no for an answer. After all that release has finally been spent comes a clear clean breath and a change of perspective. Then creation may begin. This full moon release and heal one wound at a time. Start with the personal. Mourn the loss of a loved one, a job or business. Kali can take all the anger and sorrow and turn it around. Allow her to help you release to the point of acceptance. Not forgiveness. Not forgetfulness. Acknowledge it was real and hurt like hell. Don't run away from your feelings. Sit with them and then journal.

Build Your Altar

Colors	Indigo, deep purple, scarlet
Numerology	6 – Give your health your priority
Tarot Card	Death – Change or die
Gemstones	Topaz, tanzanite, onyx, obsidian
Plant remedy	Manzanita – Prepares the body for transformation
Fragrance	Sandalwood – Awakens your sensuality

Moon Notes

Full Moon 7° Scorpio 06'
Full Moons are about moving beyond blocks and setting yourself free.

Element
Water – Taking the path of least resistance, going with the flow, secretive, sensual, glamorous, psychic, magnetic, escaping reality, a healer, an actor/actress, and creativity at its best.

Statement I Transform

Body Reproductive Organs

Mind Sex

Spirit Transformation

12th House Moon I Trust/I Transform

Umbrella Energy
How you deal with your karma, unconscious software, and what you will experience in order to attain mastery to complete your karma. It is also about the way you connect to the Divine.

Karmic Awakening Fantasy/Reality

Choice Points
Action   Profound Insights
Non-action   Isolation

Sabian Symbol
A Calm Lake Bathed In Moonlight.

Potential
A more deeply nurturing feeling is coming to life.

Clearing the Slate

Sixty hours before the full moon negative traits connected to the astro-sign might become activated to trigger what needs to be released during the full moon phase. You may notice a deep desire to be secretive, resist sharing money, a feeling of revenge, or the need to create control dramas. Make a list, look in the mirror, and for each negative trait, tell yourself *I am sorry, I forgive you, thank you for your awareness,* and *I love you.* Now is the time to start doing your Sky Power Yoga poses so your physiology can feel supported during this moon phase. The poses and the teaching are available on BlueMoonAcademy.com. Enjoy!

Scorpio Victories & Challenges

Say all of the statements in this section out loud. Then, underline the phrase that means the most to you. Use the phrase as your affirmation for releasing throughout this moon phase.

I will not compromise myself today. I know that transformation occurs when I stand tall in my truth, even if everything around me needs to die. I see death as a new beginning and know that in death comes new aliveness. I am willing to embrace transformation and open to the idea that change is in my favor. I know that in letting go, I give new life to myself. I am willing to accept that life is ever-changing and in a constant state of renewal; one cannot occur without the other.

Releasing is easy when I offer myself something new. When I allow for the motion of change to stay alive, I let go with one hand and receive with the other hand. The ever-present flow and motion keeps me alive and connected to the revitalizing power of Nature. When the power of Nature becomes apparent to me, I become aware that Nature abhors a vacuum. Rejuvenation is mine when I embrace change.

Scorpio Homework

The Scorpio moon creates the urge within us to make life happen. Pay attention to these urges so you can prepare yourself for greater action, intention, and purpose.

Gratitude List

Keep this list active throughout the moon cycle. This will bring you to a level of completion so that a new cycle of opportunity can occur in your life. Be prepared for miracles!

Tarot

Ask the question out loud, then draw a card. You may wish to draw it or paste a copy of it here. Then write down what you feel it might be telling you, in response to the question. Use the glossary in the appendix and record here anything about the card that captures your attention. You may wish to come back throughout the moon cycle to meditate or journal more on the card.

How is my heart supporting my releasing?

Releasing List

Say this statement out loud three times before writing your list:

I am a free spiritual being and it is my desire to be free to think and to express myself fully.

I am now free and ready to make choices beyond survival!

Scorpio Freedom Ideas

Now is the time to activate a game change in my life, and give up resentment, jealousy, revenge, vendettas, betrayals, blocks to transformation, destructive relationships, unhealthy joint financial situations, obstacles to having a healthy sex life, resistance to changing paradigms, and karma relating to all issues of power.

Full Moon in Scorpio

Your Personal Moon Experience

Fill in the Cosmic Check-In page. Then look up the Moon in the chart below. Take note of the "I" statement on the outside of the wheel where the Moon is located. This is the house the Moon is in, and the statement gives you the atmospheric energy, or the "umbrella energy" of this moon phase. This becomes the first statement to use in your mantra. Then, the "I" statement that corresponds with the astrological sign the Moon is in becomes the second statement (see *Moon Notes* for this moon phase). Now, locate the same sign and degree in your personal Natal chart and make a note of the house this degree falls in. The statement that corresponds with this house becomes your third statement. Go back to the Cosmic Check-In page and circle the three statements from the charts and read what you wrote. This will give you an idea about what to expect from this moon phase on a personal level. There is a video class that shows you how to read your personal chart at www.BlueMoonAcademy.com, look for *How to Use the Moon Book*.

I Trust, I Transform, I _____ .

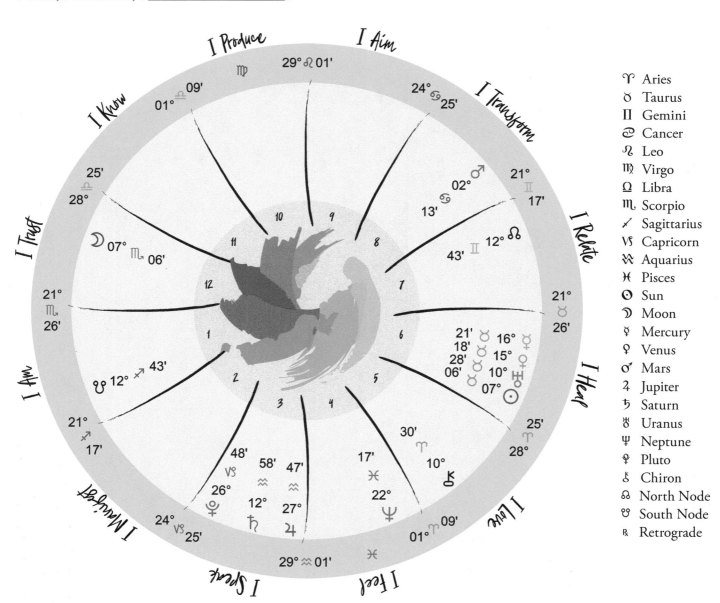

♈	Aries
♉	Taurus
♊	Gemini
♋	Cancer
♌	Leo
♍	Virgo
♎	Libra
♏	Scorpio
♐	Sagittarius
♑	Capricorn
♒	Aquarius
♓	Pisces
☉	Sun
☽	Moon
☿	Mercury
♀	Venus
♂	Mars
♃	Jupiter
♄	Saturn
♅	Uranus
♆	Neptune
♇	Pluto
⚷	Chiron
☊	North Node
☋	South Node
℞	Retrograde

Cosmic Check-In

Take a moment to write a brief phrase for each "I" statement. This activates all areas of your life for this creative cycle.

♏ I Transform

♐ I Aim

♑ I Produce

♒ I Know

♓ I Trust

♈ I Am

♉ I Manifest

♊ I Speak

♋ I Feel

♌ I Love

♍ I Heal

♎ I Relate

May

May 1st Pluto continues to be retrograde in Capricorn until October 6th

Since Pluto is at this degree for most of the year, I thought a different look at this position would be of interest. The Sabian Symbol for this retrograde is, "Pilgrims Climbing The Steep Steps Leading To A Mountain Shrine." What this means to me is that the new direction we are walking is steep, yet it takes us to a new spiritual level.

May 3rd Mercury enters Gemini

Expect to be very talkative at this time. Being in groups where new thought flows freely could lead to wonderful awareness and innovation that makes new frontiers available.

May 8th Venus enters Gemini

Time to Flirt ... expect to feel on top of your game where being charming and charmed are in alignment!

May 11th North Node, Mercury, and Uranus are tripled in Taurus during New Moon in Taurus

Expect a major download from the Universe on an idea level adding to the quality of the whole earth experience! Intelligence codes will be integrating on a corporeal level motivating advancement on the planet!

May 13th Jupiter enters Pisces

Jupiter lands in his home base and amplifies all that is good in life and heals all that needs healing. Expect blessings and expansion on all levels. The angels get activated here. My advice is to allow it and accept it!

May 20th The Sun enters Gemini

Time to get your message into the marketplace. Salesmanship goes to the front of the line right now! Use the energy of the messenger to market your ideas. This is a great time to write a blog, start a YouTube channel, create a photo book, or start a discussion, networking group, or a book club.

May 23rd Saturn goes retrograde in Aquarius until October 10th

This can lead to an intense overview of any humanitarian organization to see if the integrity of the group is a good match for you. Expect to do really thorough research on this or any other cause you have chosen.

May 26th Venus and Mercury conjunct in Gemini

Expect to hear a lot of complaining. It seems like everything is wrong and you may not be able to keep the lid on your feelings. Brat attacks are expected. Remember complaining destroys creativity. When immediate gratification is in the energy field and not satisfied, watch out!

May 29th Mercury goes retrograde in Gemini until the 29th of June

This is a time to correct miscommunications. Do what you can to avoid making decisions during this retrograde. Wait it out by looking for options. Avoid buying any new high-tech items or mechanical things like a car at this time. Don't start any travel plans. If you are traveling during this time expect delays.

Low Vitality May 2nd-4th and 13th-14th

On the 2nd through the 4th expect exhaustion from mental overload and avoid the windshield wipers of the mind. If you can't make up your mind in three minutes, let it go. On the 13th and 14th get rest and nurture yourself.

Super Sensitivity May 26th and 27th

Heightened sensitivity due to the fact that the full moon and the lunar eclipse in Sagittarius are happening at the same time. Both the eclipse and full moon require a 19-year let go, creating a great time to feel freedom.

SUNDAY	MONDAY	TUESDAY	WEDNESDAY	THURSDAY	FRIDAY	SATURDAY
						1 ♇℞ 11. A day for unconditional love.
2 ♇℞▼ ☽ V/C 7:37 AM ☽→♒ 12:31 PM 3. A beautiful day for a bike ride.	**3** ♇℞▼ ☿→♊ 7:49 PM 4. Organize your priorities.	**4** ♇℞▼ ☽ V/C 5:05 PM ☽→♓ 7:09 PM 5. Today may ask you to do a reset.	**5** ♇℞ **Cinco de Mayo** 6. Set the stage for romance.	**6** ♇℞ 7. Peace comes in quiet introspection.	**7** ♇℞ ☽ V/C 12:36 AM ☽→♈ 4:53 AM 8. Leadership comes naturally today.	**8** ♇℞ ♀→♊ 7:01 PM 9. Let someone cut in line.
9 ♇℞ **Mother's Day** ☽ V/C 3:49 PM ☽→♉ 4:47 PM 10. Look on the bright side of life.	**10** ♇℞ 11. Watch for spontaneous insights.	**11** ♇℞ **Ramadan Ends at Sunset** ● 21° ♉ 18' 12:00 PM 3. Turn up the music and dance.	**12** ♇℞ ☽ V/C 5:23 AM ☽→♊ 5:43 AM 4. Know that structure rules the day.	**13** ♇℞▼ ♃→♓ 3:36 PM 5. Today supports easy action.	**14** ♇℞▼ ☽ V/C 3:50 AM ☽→♋ 6:31 PM 6. Listen with love.	**15** ♇℞ 7. Share one of your favorite books.
16 ♇℞ ☽ V/C 11:22 PM 8. What is moving towards you?	**17** ♇℞ ☽→♌ 5:44 PM 9. Does a neighbor need your help?	**18** ♇℞ 10. A new beginning is available.	**19** ♇℞ ☽ V/C 12:12 PM ☽→♍ 2:00 PM 11. The Universe has your back.	**20** ♇℞ ☉→♊ 12:37 PM 3. Get out the paints and crayons.	**21** ♇℞ ☽ V/C 12:55 PM ☽→♎ 6:36 PM 4. Appreciate trustworthiness.	**22** ♇℞ 5. Notice progressive attitudes.
23 ♄♇℞ ♄℞ 13° ♒ 31' 2:19 AM ☽ V/C 2:36 PM ☽→♏ 8:00 PM 6. Light the candles for romance.	**24** ♄♇℞ 7. Explore new ideas.	**25** ♄♇℞ ☽ V/C 2:19 PM ☽→♐ 7:39 PM 8. Believe prosperity is always yours.	**26** ♄♇℞▲ ○ 5° ♐ 26' 4:14 AM **Lunar Eclipse** 5° ♐ 29' 4:19 AM 9. Spirit is waiting to listen to you.	**27** ♄♇℞▲ ☽ V/C 10:35 AM ☽→♑ 7:23 PM 11. Empower greatness in others.	**28** ♄♇℞ 3. Be social, have a cocktail party.	**29** ☿♄♇℞ ☽ V/C 3:14 PM ☿℞ 24° ♊ 43' 3:34 PM ☽→♒ 9:04 PM 4. Can you see how loyalty is a benefit?
30 ☿♄♇℞ 5. What peaks your curiosity?	**31** ☿♄♇℞ **Memorial Day** ☽ V/C 11:13 PM 6. Spend time in your garden.					

♈ Aries	♍ Virgo	♒ Aquarius	♀ Venus	♆ Neptune	V/C Void-of-Course	2. Balance	7. Learning
♉ Taurus	♎ Libra	♓ Pisces	♂ Mars	♇ Pluto	℞ Retrograde	3. Fun	8. Money
♊ Gemini	♏ Scorpio	☉ Sun	♃ Jupiter	→ Enters	S͞D Stationary Direct	4. Structure	9. Spirituality
♋ Cancer	♐ Sagittarius	☽ Moon	♄ Saturn	● New Moon	▲ Super Sensitivity	5. Action	10. Visionary
♌ Leo	♑ Capricorn	☿ Mercury	♅ Uranus	○ Full Moon	▼ Low Vitality	6. Love	11. Completion

New Moon in Taurus

May 11th, 12:00 PM

When the Sun is in Taurus

Taurus is the time when we see the true manifesting power, as the plants move to a higher aspiration of life and bloom. Once again, we become connected to the essence of beauty as a symbol of our divinity. Taurus is the connection between humanity and divinity. Taurus' job is to infuse matter with light through accumulating layers of substance. This is why they are such good shoppers and collectors. The more they accumulate, the more divinity they experience. This process brings about a sense of self-value which is directly commensurate to the amount of money they manifest. Personal resources are part of the pattern. Discover your value at this time.

Taurus Goddess

With glitter and gold, sumptuous silks of red, and sensuous earthy drumbeats, Aphrodite belly dances into your life this moon, to remind you of embodied joy. Her hand reaches yours and pulls you on the dance floor, asking you to 'wo-manifest' your dreams. Creation requires heart-felt emotion from deep in your core. Music and dance can be your fastest route to your feelings. As Goddess of passion, one of Aphrodite's epithets was "Smile-loving." Adaptation necessitated changing cherished traditions in 2020, it kept us apart from families and friends, and cancelled our favorite past-times. It shocked us with its abruptness. But at the same time, it also brought us back into our homes and eliminated the mindless rushing from event to event. Work-Life balance shifted radically. We took time to breathe and to appreciate our loved ones and our homes; no longer taking anything for granted. Suddenly, for some, there was more time to enjoy the company of children, elders, and pets. For others, those simple pleasures may have disappeared through illness, death or separation. Aphrodite brings the promise of love and bliss into your new moon manifestation ritual. Imagine bringing the "Smile-Loving" Aphrodite's elements into your home to make closeness, security and peace your priority and a tangible reality.

Build Your Altar

Colors	Green, pink, deep red, earth tones
Numerology	3 – Turn up the music and dance
Tarot Card	Hierophant – The interpreter of life
Gemstones	Topaz, agate, smoky quartz, jade, rose quartz
Plant Remedy	Angelica – Connecting Heaven and Earth
Fragrance	Rose – Opening the heart

Moon Notes

New Moon   21° Taurus 18'
New Moons are about opening new pathways for prosperity.

Element
Earth – Practical, determined, structured, enduring, stubborn, traditional, stable, and stuck inside the box.

Statement   I Manifest

Body   Neck

Mind   Collecting

Spirit   Manifestation

10th House Moon   I Produce/I Manifest

Umbrella Energy
Your approach to status, career, honor, and prestige, and why you chose your father.

Choice Points
Action   Discernment
Non-action   Blind Obedience

Sabian Symbol
A White Dove Flying Over Troubled Waters.

Potential
Good news about peace coming our way.

Taurus Victories & Challenges

Say all of the statements in this section out loud. Then, under-line the phrase that means the most to you. Use the phrase as your affirmation for manifesting throughout this moon phase.

Everything is possible for me today. My possibilities are endless. I have the power within me to make all of my dreams come true. I have the tools to make my talent a reality. I have the power to identify with my talent. Today, I focus my attention and intention on manifesting with my talent and, in so doing, I transform my ideas into reality. I recognize the part of me that is connected to the cosmic source of ideas and I express that source within me to manifest my creative power. I see my possibilities and act on them today. I am the creative power. I am all-knowing. I am an individual. There is no one else like me. I can manifest anything I desire. I intend it, I allow it, so be it.

Rules for Manifesting

Know what you want. Write it down. Say it out loud. Recognize that because you thought it, it can be so. Release your limiting beliefs. Override your limiting beliefs with power statements. Act as if you have already manifested your idea. Lastly, value yourself!

Taurus Homework

Taureans manifest best when buying, selling, and owning real estate, gardening and landscaping, selling and collecting art, manufacturing and selling fine furniture, singing or acting, and as a restaurateur, antique dealer, or interior designer.

The Taurus moon asks us to infuse light into form and, in so doing, the bridge between humanity and divinity is actualized and we can assume our stewardship in the physical world. When we release Spirit into matter, we become open to the idea that accumulation and actualization set us free to experience the abundance available to us here on Earth. Go shopping!

Victory List

Acknowledge what you have overcome. Keep this list active during this moon cycle. Honoring victory allows you to accept success.

Tarot

Ask the question out loud, then draw a card. You may wish to draw it or paste a copy of it here. Then write down what you feel it might be telling you, in response to the question. Use the glossary in the appendix and record here anything about the card that captures your attention. You may wish to come back throughout the moon cycle to meditate or journal more on the card.

How is my body supporting my manifesting?

Manifesting List

This or something better than this comes to me in an easy and pleasurable way, for the good of all concerned. Thank you, Universe!

Taurus Manifesting Ideas

Now is the time to focus on manifesting success, money, property, luxury, beauty, personal value, and pleasure.

New Moon in Taurus

Your Personal Moon Experience

Fill in the Cosmic Check-In page. Then look up the Moon in the chart below. Take note of the "I" statement on the outside of the wheel where the Moon is located. This is the house the Moon is in, and the statement gives you the atmospheric energy, or the "umbrella energy" of this moon phase. This becomes the first statement to use in your mantra. Then, the "I" statement that corresponds with the astrological sign the Moon is in becomes the second statement (see *Moon Notes* for this moon phase). Now, locate the same sign and degree in your personal Natal chart and make a note of the house this degree falls in. The statement that corresponds with this house becomes your third statement. Go back to the Cosmic Check-In page and circle the three statements from the charts and read what you wrote. This will give you an idea about what to expect from this moon phase on a personal level. There is a video class that shows you how to read your personal chart at www.BlueMoonAcademy.com, look for *How to Use the Moon Book*.

I Produce, I Manifest, I _____ .

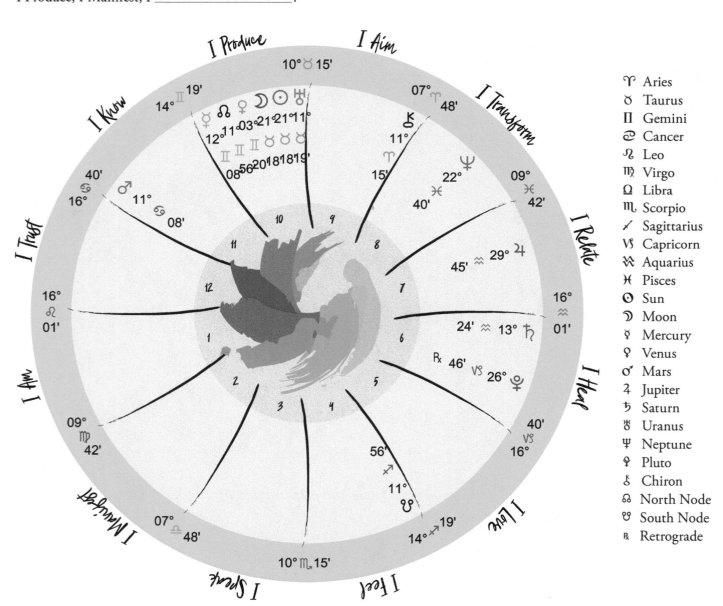

♈	Aries
♉	Taurus
♊	Gemini
♋	Cancer
♌	Leo
♍	Virgo
♎	Libra
♏	Scorpio
♐	Sagittarius
♑	Capricorn
♒	Aquarius
♓	Pisces
☉	Sun
☽	Moon
☿	Mercury
♀	Venus
♂	Mars
♃	Jupiter
♄	Saturn
♅	Uranus
♆	Neptune
♇	Pluto
⚷	Chiron
☊	North Node
☋	South Node
℞	Retrograde

Cosmic Check-In

Taurus New Moon
May 11th, 12:00 PM

Take a moment to write a brief phrase for each "I" statement. This activates all areas of your life for this creative cycle.

♉ I Manifest

♊ I Speak

♋ I Feel

♌ I Love

♍ I Heal

♎ I Relate

♏ I Transform

♐ I Aim

♑ I Produce

♒ I Know

♓ I Trust

♈ I Am

Full Moon in Sagittarius

May 26th, 4:14 AM

When the Sun is Opposite the Moon

Full moons are always in opposition to the Sun. This creates a feeling of tension between where you want to shine and how your feelings are flowing on a sensory level about the Sun's directive. The two forces seem like they are working against each other, yet they are on the same team displaying different techniques to obtain the same mission. The Sagittarius/Gemini polarity creates tension between the quest for higher knowledge and the need for academic accolades.

Sagittarius Goddess

Self-expression is Saraswati's domain. Her name is derived from Sara meaning 'essence' and sva meaning 'self.' A river goddess, Saraswati brings the flow of inspiration for any creative endeavor, from dance to writing to art. She is knowledge and wisdom personified, as well as a world-traveler familiar with many cultures, beliefs and ways of being. One of the things that massive change brings us is the opportunity to do things differently; to take a chance on a new way of living and loving. Know that your power comes from what you learned and experienced; how you adapted and persevered. Saraswati can help you unlock your creativity to share what you hold in your heart. She can help you overcome writer's block or find the right media to reach across borders or boundaries. Saraswati's wisdom may help us all break through barriers to a greater understanding of one another, inspiring us to solve the most important issues of our time. She may teach us to repair the divisions that have pitted groups against one another. Allow Saraswati to guide your hands as you write, or paint, or dance, or interpret. Open your mind to receive her grace. Light a candle and ask Saraswati what unique story is your own to share for your own healing? And how might your story bring comfort and understanding to others?

Build Your Altar

Colors	Deep purple, turquoise, royal blue
Numerology	9 - Spirit is waiting to listen to you
Tarot Card	Temperance – Balancing the present with the past, updating yourself
Gemstone	Turquoise
Plant remedy	Madia – Seeing and hitting the target
Fragrance	Magnolia – Expanded beauty

Moon Notes

Full Moon 5° Sagittarius 26'
Full Moons are about moving beyond blocks and setting yourself free.

Lunar Eclipse 4:19 AM

Element
Fire – Igniting, dissolving, accelerating, cleansing, advancing awareness, impatience, leadership, passion, and vitality.

Statement I Aim

Body Thighs

Mind Philosophical

Spirit Optimism

7th House Moon I Relate/I Aim

Umbrella Energy
One-on-one relationships, defines your people attraction and how you work in relationships with the people you attract.

Choice Points
Action   Wise Sage
Non-action   Know-it-all

Sabian Symbol
An Old Owl Sits Alone On The Branch Of A Large Tree.

Potential
Take a time-out to gather wisdom.

Clearing the Slate

Sixty hours before the full moon negative traits connected to the astro-sign might become activated to trigger what needs to be released during the full moon phase. You may notice a sudden urge to be excessive, to resist reality by exaggerating, to speak before thinking, to be blunt, or to use unfiltered language. Make a list, look in the mirror, and for each negative trait, tell yourself *I am sorry, I forgive you, thank you for your awareness,* and *I love you.* Now is the time to start doing your Sky Power Yoga poses so your physiology can feel supported during this moon phase. The poses and the teaching are available on BlueMoonAcademy.com. Enjoy!

Sagittarius Victories & Challenges

Say all of the statements in this section out loud. Then, underline the phrase that means the most to you. Use the phrase as your affirmation for releasing throughout this moon phase.

Today, I blend my old self with my new self, my physical reality with my spiritual awareness, my positive thoughts with my negative thoughts, my past with my present, my feminine with my masculine, my rewards with my losses, my ups with my downs, and my higher self with my lower self. It is a day for me to refine and fine tune my life by looking at my extremes. I recognize what inspires me and what keeps me stuck. I find my center today by acknowledging my extremes. I am aware that balance comes to those who are able to locate the space in the center of these opposite energy fields. When I am in my center, my polarities are in motion. Healing cannot occur unless my polarities are moving and I know that healing is motion.

I am ready for a healing today and know that by visiting my opposites and determining their vast opposition to each other, I can find the paradoxes that I have chosen for myself and begin to heal. I am willing to experiment with this blending of opposites and become the alchemist of my own life. When I blend all aspects of myself, rather than separating them, I can truly become whole. Today is a day to integrate, rather than separate, in order to release the spark of light that stays prisoner when my polarities are in operation. When I find balance, motion occurs and the Law of Harmony takes over, putting paradoxical energies to rest, thus breaking the crystallization of polarity. The Law of Harmony is beauty in motion, promoting the flow of color, light, sound, and movement into form. Balance is a condition that keeps my spark in motion. I become the vertical line in the center of polarity today and carry the secret of balance. Balance cannot be my goal, motion is my goal today. When I am in motion, I can take action to evolve and to express all of myself freely.

Sagittarius Homework

Now is the time to use your physical body to release the feeling of being caged in by people or circumstances. Choose an activity that burns away confinement and allows you to feel the power of your passion.

The Sagittarius moon awakens us to know the spark of light that lives in our heart, thus elevating love in ourselves and in our world. This is when we come to realize what is in our highest and best good and we can begin to recalibrate all that is not lovable in our lives.

Gratitude List

Keep this list active throughout the moon cycle. This will bring you to a level of completion so that a new cycle of opportunity can occur in your life. Be prepared for miracles!

Tarot

Ask the question out loud, then draw a card. You may wish to draw it or paste a copy of it here. Then write down what you feel it might be telling you, in response to the question. Use the glossary in the appendix and record here anything about the card that captures your attention. You may wish to come back throughout the moon cycle to meditate or journal more on the card.

How is my spirit supporting my releasing?

Releasing List

Say this statement out loud three times before writing your list:

I am a free spiritual being and it is my desire to be free to think and to express myself fully.

I am now free and ready to make choices beyond survival!

Sagittarius Freedom Ideas

Now is the time to activate a game change in my life, and give up belief systems that no longer apply, attitudes that are not uplifting to me, addiction to excess and risk, the need to exaggerate based on low self-esteem, dishonesty, being too blunt, staying in the future and avoiding the NOW, overriding fear by being too optimistic, and preaching.

Full Moon in Sagittarius

Your Personal Moon Experience

Fill in the Cosmic Check-In page. Then look up the Moon in the chart below. Take note of the "I" statement on the outside of the wheel where the Moon is located. This is the house the Moon is in, and the statement gives you the atmospheric energy, or the "umbrella energy" of this moon phase. This becomes the first statement to use in your mantra. Then, the "I" statement that corresponds with the astrological sign the Moon is in becomes the second statement (see *Moon Notes* for this moon phase). Now, locate the same sign and degree in your personal Natal chart and make a note of the house this degree falls in. The statement that corresponds with this house becomes your third statement. Go back to the Cosmic Check-In page and circle the three statements from the charts and read what you wrote. This will give you an idea about what to expect from this moon phase on a personal level. There is a video class that shows you how to read your personal chart at www.BlueMoonAcademy.com, look for *How to Use the Moon Book*.

I Relate, I Aim, I _____ .

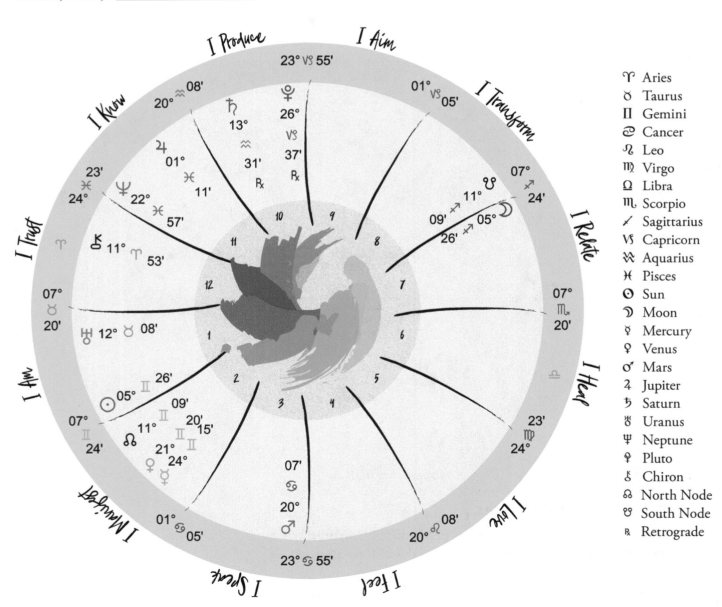

♈	Aries
♉	Taurus
♊	Gemini
♋	Cancer
♌	Leo
♍	Virgo
♎	Libra
♏	Scorpio
♐	Sagittarius
♑	Capricorn
♒	Aquarius
♓	Pisces
☉	Sun
☽	Moon
☿	Mercury
♀	Venus
♂	Mars
♃	Jupiter
♄	Saturn
♅	Uranus
♆	Neptune
♇	Pluto
⚷	Chiron
☊	North Node
☋	South Node
℞	Retrograde

Cosmic Check-In

Sagittarius Full Moon
May 26th, 4:14 AM

Take a moment to write a brief phrase for each "I" statement. This activates all areas of your life for this creative cycle.

♐ I Aim

♑ I Produce

♒ I Know

♓ I Trust

♈ I Am

♉ I Manifest

♊ I Speak

♋ I Feel

♌ I Love

♍ I Heal

♎ I Relate

♏ I Transform

June

June 1st Mercury Retrograde in Gemini until the 22nd of the month

Time to make amends where miscommunications have hindered your consciousness by spending too much time on your past.

June 1st Saturn Retrograde in Aquarius for the entire month

Time to resolve issues relating to any group consciousness that doesn't match your integrity. Research is the best use of your mind at this time.

June 1st Pluto Retrograde for the entire month

Look for unresolved issues relating to your finances. Get with a consultant to determine the right action around your money.

June 11th Mars enters Leo

Oh dear! This can bring on highly competitive surges. The need to be top dog can create severe conflict unless controlled. Best to come from your heart rather than your ego and all will be well.

June 20th Jupiter goes Retrograde in Pisces for the rest of the month

This brings on a 12-year review. Jupiter rules home, health, and happiness in love relationships. You may feel like you are watching re-runs of your life at this time. The question to ask yourself is, "What was I up to around home, health, and happiness in 2009?" Time to make amends with yourself and ask what will it take to reset yourself now.

June 25th Neptune goes retrograde in Pisces

This is a time when illusions or distorted fantasies can interfere with your life. Remember Pisces loves fantasy and Neptune can create delusions about those fantasies. This is a good time to do a reality check so you don't fall into the 'smoke and mirrors' prone to this retrograde. Watch out for your addiction coming up to keep you from feeling the effects of the truth.

June 26th Venus enters Leo

Party time! Expect to have urges to dance on the table tops and have deep creative expressions, such as shopping, redecorating your home, going to dance class, theatre class, or singing in the chorus or at karaoke.

Low Vitality June 1st-4th, 9th-10th, and 18th-19th

On the 1st through the 4th Venus is over the Low Vitality field. Worry and complaining could really take you down. On the 9th and 10th, sharing the space with a solar eclipse and new moon in Gemini could bring about self-doubt that can exhaust you. Stick with the power of the new moon by writing a major manifesting list! On the 18th and 19th get rest.

Super Sensitivity June 23 and 24th

Lots of chaotic activity in the sky; it is universal, not personal. Keep strong boundaries around your thoughts and all will be well!

SUNDAY	MONDAY	TUESDAY	WEDNESDAY	THURSDAY	FRIDAY	SATURDAY
		1 ☿♄♀ᴿ▼ ☽→♓ 2:08 AM 7. Have faith in how much you know.	**2** ☿♄♀ᴿ▼ ♀→♋ 6:18 AM 8. Success means staying on purpose.	**3** ☿♄♀ᴿ▼ ☽ V/C 4:10 AM ☽→♈ 10:59 AM 9. See the Divine Grace within.	**4** ☿♄♀ᴿ▼ 10. Combine the new tech with old.	**5** ☿♄♀ᴿ ☽ V/C 3:46 PM ☽→♉ 10:47 PM 11. Look around with wonder.
6 ☿♄♀ᴿ 3. Complements build self-esteem.	**7** ☿♄♀ᴿ 4. A 'follow the directions' day.	**8** ☿♄♀ᴿ ☽ V/C 8:06 AM ☽→♊ 11:48 AM 5. Answers come when you move.	**9** ☿♄♀ᴿ▼ 6. Light a candle, breathe in love.	**10** ☿♄♀ᴿ▼ Solar Eclipse 19° ♊ 42' 3:42 AM ● 19° ♊ 47' 3:53 AM ☽ V/C 10:37 AM 7. What's new on the scientific front?	**11** ☿♄♀ᴿ ♂→♌ 6:34 AM ☽→♋ 12:23 AM 8. Make money your friend.	**12** ☿♄♀ᴿ 9. Find harmony through meditation.
13 ☿♄♀ᴿ ☽ V/C 4:15 AM ☽→♌ 11:23 AM 10. Have your goals become victories?	**14** ☿♄♀ᴿ Flag Day 11. Close your eyes, feel the wholeness.	**15** ☿♄♀ᴿ ☽ V/C 10:27 AM ☽→♍ 8:01 PM 3. Go out and play.	**16** ☿♄♀ᴿ 4. A solid foundation is needed.	**17** ☿♄♀ᴿ ☽ V/C 8:54 PM 5. Take a new route to a familiar place.	**18** ☿♄♀ᴿ▼ ☽→♎ 1:54 AM 6. Pamper your feet today.	**19** ☿♄♀ᴿ▼ 7. Wisdom appears in a surprising way.
20 ☿♃♄♀ᴿ Father's Day ☽ V/C 3:51 AM ☽→♏ 4:58 AM ♃ᴿ 20° ♓ 11' 8:05 AM Summer Solstice ☉→♋ 8:32 PM 8. Honor your successes today.	**21** ☿♃♄♀ᴿ ☽ V/C 11:43 PM 9. Give to a noteworthy cause.	**22** ♃♄♀ᴿ ☽→♐ 5:56 AM ☿ᴰˢ 16° ♊ 08' 3:00 PM 10. Acknowledge idealism today.	**23** ♃♄♀ᴿ▲ ☽ V/C 7:08 PM 11. Trust your knowing.	**24** ♃♄♀ᴿ▲ ☽→♑ 6:05 AM ○ 3° ♑ 28' 11:39 AM 3. Plan to attend a social event.	**25** ♃♄♆♀ᴿ ♆ᴿ 23° ♓ 12' 12:22 PM 4. Let the plan be to create ease.	**26** ♃♄♆♀ᴿ ☽ V/C 5:49 AM ☽→♒ 7:09 AM ♀→♌ 9:27 PM 5. How many options are open?
27 ♃♄♆♀ᴿ ☽ V/C 12:07 PM 6. Trust love, it's the divine plan.	**28** ♃♄♆♀ᴿ ☽→♓ 10:50 AM 7. Life's mysteries are unfolding daily.	**29** ♃♄♆♀ᴿ 8. You are your own authority.	**30** ♃♄♆♀ᴿ ☽ V/C 10:39 AM ☽→♈ 6:22 PM 9. Pray with gratitude.			

♈ Aries	♍ Virgo	♒ Aquarius	♀ Venus	♆ Neptune	V/C Void-of-Course	2. Balance	7. Learning
♉ Taurus	♎ Libra	♓ Pisces	♂ Mars	♇ Pluto	ᴿ Retrograde	3. Fun	8. Money
♊ Gemini	♏ Scorpio	☉ Sun	♃ Jupiter	→ Enters	ᴰˢ Stationary Direct	4. Structure	9. Spirituality
♋ Cancer	♐ Sagittarius	☽ Moon	♄ Saturn	● New Moon	▲ Super Sensitivity	5. Action	10. Visionary
♌ Leo	♑ Capricorn	☿ Mercury	♅ Uranus	○ Full Moon	▼ Low Vitality	6. Love	11. Completion

New Moon in Gemini

June 10th, 3:53 AM

When the Sun is in Gemini

This is a time when the ability to communicate is at the top of the priority list. Allow your thoughts to lead you to a formula for success so you can put your thoughts into action. Then, find the appropriate soapbox to stand on so your message can be heard. Now is the time to make your message clear, enlightening, witty, and thought-provoking. Your bright mind is on its high throne and waiting for an audience. Try blogging, do a show on YouTube, join Toastmasters, write that screenplay, film yourself doing a travel show, start a discussion group, or write a newsletter for your neighborhood. Most of all, put your bright mind to work!

Gemini Goddess

Iris, the Rainbow Messenger, appears this moon on golden wings, bringing a heliogram from the Gods. She rides the arc of the rainbow, fulfilling prayers for the re-establishment of hope. It was said that a rainbow only appeared long enough for Iris to bring her messages and then return to the heavens. She was known as a conciliator, the one who restored the peace in contentious situations. As we approach summer solstice, this new moon, Iris glides in, with hope in hand. The next time "Somewhere Over the Rainbow" plays unexpectedly, stop and pay attention; especially the version by Israel Kamakawiwo'ole that includes lyrics from "What a Wonderful World." Iris is nearby bringing peace to someone. Allow yourself a few minutes to daydream about peace, prosperity and opening new pathways for opportunity to flow to you.

One year ago today, George Floyd was laid to rest in Houston, Texas. Of the many statements in eulogies, we find Iris's message, that has been echoed through the ages. One of the many versions of the quote, from a sermon by Rev. Seth Brooks in a 1934 sermon in Malden, Massachusetts, adds the Iris touch, "We must believe that the arc of the universe is long, but that it bends toward justice, toward one Divine end, towards which creation moves onward and onward, forever." Let us pause today and pray for a more just and loving world.

Build Your Altar

Colors	Bright yellow, orange, multi-colors
Numerology	7 – What's new on the scientific front?
Tarot Card	The Lovers – Integrate, don't separate
Gemstones	Yellow diamond, citrine
Plant Remedy	Morning Glory – Thinking with your heart.
Fragrance	Iris – The ability to focus the mind

Moon Notes

New Moon 19° Gemini 47'
New Moons are about opening new pathways for prosperity.

Solar Eclipse 3:42 AM

Element
Air – The breath of life that allows the mind to achieve new insights and fresh perspectives, abstract dreaming, freedom from attachments, codes of intelligence, and academic applications.

Statement I Speak

Body Hands and Lungs

Mind Analytical

Spirit Messenger

2nd House Moon I Manifest/I Speak

Umbrella Energy
The way you make your money and the way you spend your money.

Choice Points
Action	Quality
Non-action	Quantity

Sabian Symbol
A Modern Cafeteria Displays An Abundance Of Food, Products Of Various Regions.

Potential
Accepting gifts from the Earth.

Gemini Victories & Challenges

Say all of the statements in this section out loud. Then, underline the phrase that means the most to you. Use the phrase as your affirmation for manifesting throughout this moon phase.

I am dark. I am light. I am day. I am night. The extremes in life exist within me, completing themselves in reality. The "I" that is "we" lives within me. I am one in the same. I am both.

I know that flow comes from accepting my opposite natures. Today, I accept my opposites and get into the flow. I am aware today of how my judgments separate me from people, events, experiences, and, most of all, from myself. Today, I am going to see where I have separated all of the parts of myself and begin to integrate into wholeness through acceptance and understanding. I begin by breathing. I breathe in wholeness and breathe out separation. I understand that breath is life and that life includes all facets of my experience to gain awareness. I know that I am Heaven. I know that I am Earth. I know that I am masculine. I know that I am feminine. Today, I become unified. Today, I integrate into wholeness. I breathe into all of these aspects of myself, knowing that in my totality I am connected to Oneness. The "I" that is "we" lives within me. I am one in the same. I am both.

Gemini Homework

Geminis manifest best through broadcasting and journalism, as a speech coach, comedian, political satirist, gossip columnist, negotiator, media specialist, manicurist, salesperson, teacher, or travel consultant.

Expect to awaken your will on seven levels…

- The will to direct – through the power of your original intention.

- The will to love – stimulating goodwill among humankind through cooperation.

- The will to act – by laying foundations for a happier world.

- The will to cooperate – the desire and demand for right relationships.

- The will to know – to think correctly and creatively so that every man/woman can find their outstanding characteristics.

- The will to persist – to be one with your light and represent the ideal standard for living.

- The will to organize – to carry forward direct inspiration through groups of goodwill.

Victory List

Acknowledge what you have overcome. Keep this list active during this moon cycle. Honoring victory allows you to accept success.

Tarot

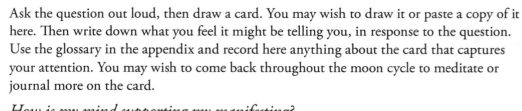

Ask the question out loud, then draw a card. You may wish to draw it or paste a copy of it here. Then write down what you feel it might be telling you, in response to the question. Use the glossary in the appendix and record here anything about the card that captures your attention. You may wish to come back throughout the moon cycle to meditate or journal more on the card.

How is my mind supporting my manifesting?

Manifesting List

This or something better than this comes to me in an easy and pleasurable way, for the good of all concerned. Thank you, Universe!

Gemini Manifesting Ideas

Now is the time to focus on manifesting communications, a promotion, technology, ideas, non-judgmental communication, thinking outside of duality, a quiet mind, charisma and charm, and flirting.

New Moon in Gemini

Your Personal Moon Experience

Fill in the Cosmic Check-In page. Then look up the Moon in the chart below. Take note of the "I" statement on the outside of the wheel where the Moon is located. This is the house the Moon is in, and the statement gives you the atmospheric energy, or the "umbrella energy" of this moon phase. This becomes the first statement to use in your mantra. Then, the "I" statement that corresponds with the astrological sign the Moon is in becomes the second statement (see *Moon Notes* for this moon phase). Now, locate the same sign and degree in your personal Natal chart and make a note of the house this degree falls in. The statement that corresponds with this house becomes your third statement. Go back to the Cosmic Check-In page and circle the three statements from the charts and read what you wrote. This will give you an idea about what to expect from this moon phase on a personal level. There is a video class that shows you how to read your personal chart at www.BlueMoonAcademy.com, look for *How to Use the Moon Book*.

I Manifest, I Speak, I _____ .

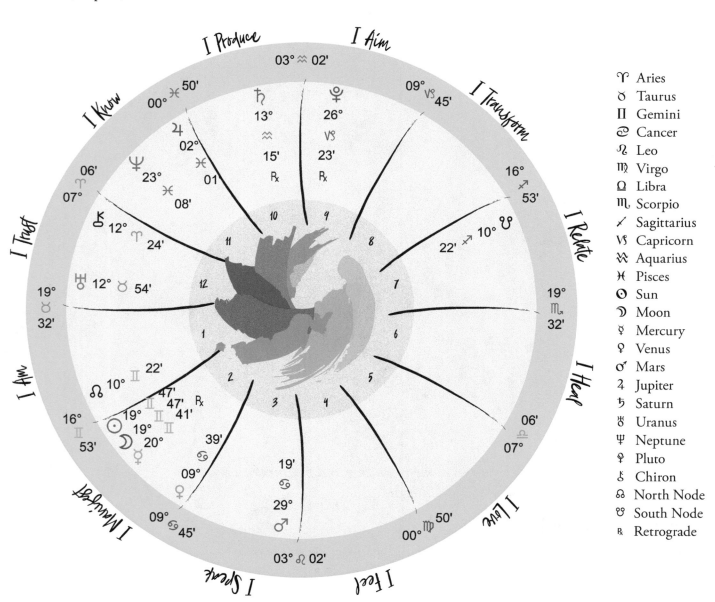

♈	Aries
♉	Taurus
♊	Gemini
♋	Cancer
♌	Leo
♍	Virgo
♎	Libra
♏	Scorpio
♐	Sagittarius
♑	Capricorn
♒	Aquarius
♓	Pisces
☉	Sun
☽	Moon
☿	Mercury
♀	Venus
♂	Mars
♃	Jupiter
♄	Saturn
♅	Uranus
♆	Neptune
♇	Pluto
⚷	Chiron
☊	North Node
☋	South Node
℞	Retrograde

Cosmic Check-In

Gemini New Moon
June 10th, 3:53 AM

Take a moment to write a brief phrase for each "I" statement. This activates all areas of your life for this creative cycle.

♊ I Speak

♋ I Feel

♌ I Love

♍ I Heal

♎ I Relate

♏ I Transform

♐ I Aim

♑ I Produce

♒ I Know

♓ I Trust

♈ I Am

♉ I Manifest

Full Moon in Capricorn

June 24th, 11:39 AM

When the Sun is Opposite the Moon

Full moons are always in opposition to the Sun. This creates a feeling of tension between where you want to shine and how your feelings are flowing on a sensory level about the Sun's directive. The two forces seem like they are working against each other, yet they are on the same team displaying different techniques to obtain the same mission. The Capricorn/Cancer polarity creates tension between the quest for status and the need to feel secure.

Capricorn Goddess

Reminding us of the work of tending the fields at the time of the year's longest daylight and summer's eve, Ceres ushers in the urge to be productive. A goddess of agriculture, fertility and motherly love, Ceres name was synonymous with the terms "to bear" or "bring forth". She is most often pictured with a sheaf of wheat, and her name is where our word "cereal" derives. It was Ceres' life-sustaining gift of abundance, following all the peoples' care, attention, and labor had been bestowed upon the seeds and the land. Cultivation also has other meanings beyond agriculture: to devote special attention, to court special friendship with someone, to improve oneself by study, to refine or impart culture or civilization; to discriminate in taste or refine judgment. With the light at its peak, Ceres may reveal to you new ways to raise up, to quicken or enliven your determination to cultivate all aspects of self-improvement. What is growing in light within you? To what are you paying special attention? What seeds are you tending? Mid-year is a perfect time to re-assess your progress and make any course corrections needed to keep you on track. Growth requires special conscious awareness of goals and serious concerted effort to achieve. Perhaps it is time to enlist your friends or take on a community service project to expand your sphere of influence. It might even be volunteering at a community garden or handing out provisions at a food bank, or a city beautification project. Ceres asks you to bring forth your light and produce something you will be proud to share.

Build Your Altar

Colors   Forest green, earth tones

Numerology   3 – Plan to attend a social event

Tarot Card   Devil – Time to look at the broader view

Gemstones   Smoky quartz, topaz, garnet

Plant remedy Rosemary – Activates appropriate memory

Fragrance   Frankincense – Assists the Soul's entry into the body

Moon Notes

Full Moon   3° Capricorn 28'
Full Moons are about moving beyond blocks and setting yourself free.

Element
Earth – Practical, determined, structured, enduring, stubborn, traditional, stable, and stuck inside the box.

Statement   I Produce

Body   Knees

Mind   Ambition

Spirit   Achievement

4th House Moon   I Feel/I Produce

Umbrella Energy
The way your early environmental training was and how that set your foundation for living, and why you chose your mother.

Choice Points
Action   Eagerness
Non-action   Greediness

Sabian Symbol
A Human Soul, In Its Eagerness For New Experiences, Seeks Embodiment.

Potential
Vulnerability requires space.

Clearing the Slate

Sixty hours before the full moon negative traits connected to the astro-sign might become activated to trigger what needs to be released during the full moon phase. You may notice a sudden burden of responsibility taking over your experience of life, of paying too much attention to status and position, of no time to feel compassionate, and of challenging authorities. Make a list, look in the mirror, and for each negative trait, tell yourself *I am sorry, I forgive you, thank you for your awareness,* and *I love you.* Now is the time to start doing your Sky Power Yoga poses so your physiology can feel supported during this moon phase. The poses and the teaching are available on BlueMoonAcademy.com. Enjoy!

Capricorn Victories & Challenges

Say all of the statements in this section out loud. Then, underline the phrase that means the most to you. Use the phrase as your affirmation for releasing throughout this moon phase.

I feel limited. I feel confined. I feel stuck. I feel there is no way out. Perhaps I am the target of someone's envy or jealousy, or perhaps I am jealous or I am envious. Maybe I am spending too much time in the outer world and putting too much value on material rewards, things, and possessions. Maybe I am trying to possess someone or limit their view or choice. I may feel there are no choices. Maybe I am living by someone else's rules and beliefs and forgot how to think for myself. I could also be overcome by fear and too terrorized to look at anything at all.

Today, I see and feel the limits of placing the source of love outside myself. I have tunnel vision and I seem to have forgotten to look at my options. I must ask myself today, "How many ways can I look at my life, my situation, or my perceived problems?" Today, I must expand my view to encompass 360-degrees instead of only 180-degrees. I begin by acknowledging to myself that today is the worst it is going to get. I know deep within me that if I allow myself to truly experience my bottom, the top will become visible to me. It is time to look at the brighter side. Begin by identifying the problem by writing it down on a piece of paper.

Start with the phrase, "The problem is _____." Fill in the blank. Then, list as many solutions to the problem as you can. List at least three. Then, say these solutions out loud every day until the answer comes to you through a person, an idea, an event, or a choice.

Capricorn Homework

Put on a good pair of walking shoes and get ready to walk your blues away. It is time to get outside and feel the loving power of Mother Earth. The green of the trees refreshes your stagnant energy while you exhaust yourself to a point of vulnerability. Then, and only then, will you feel freedom. Give yourself permission to throw your watch away and learn to live in the moment.

The Capricorn moon is the reincarnation of Spirit emerging from the dark waters of our past emotions releasing us from our fear of change and our fear of loss. Awaken your powerful and positive spiritual connection to be open to new possibilities. Ask yourself to release your emotional loyalty to the past. We are reminded of our need for material and emotional security at this time. In order to ensure this, we must learn to build a foundation for ourselves that is lit from within, made from the materials of love, goodwill, and intelligence.

Gratitude List

Keep this list active throughout the moon cycle. This will bring you to a level of completion so that a new cycle of opportunity can occur in your life. Be prepared for miracles!

Tarot

Ask the question out loud, then draw a card. You may wish to draw it or paste a copy of it here. Then write down what you feel it might be telling you, in response to the question. Use the glossary in the appendix and record here anything about the card that captures your attention. You may wish to come back throughout the moon cycle to meditate or journal more on the card.

How is my body supporting my releasing?

Releasing List

Say this statement out loud three times before writing your list:

I am a free spiritual being and it is my desire to be free to think and to express myself fully.

I am now free and ready to make choices beyond survival!

Capricorn Freedom Ideas

Now is the time to activate a game change in my life, and give up obstacles to success, authority issues, sorrow and sadness, fear that blocks me, arrogance, irritability, limitations of time, priorities that are no longer valid, control and domination, the need to do it all alone, and taking on excessive responsibility.

Full Moon in Capricorn

Your Personal Moon Experience

Fill in the Cosmic Check-In page. Then look up the Moon in the chart below. Take note of the "I" statement on the outside of the wheel where the Moon is located. This is the house the Moon is in, and the statement gives you the atmospheric energy, or the "umbrella energy" of this moon phase. This becomes the first statement to use in your mantra. Then, the "I" statement that corresponds with the astrological sign the Moon is in becomes the second statement (see *Moon Notes* for this moon phase). Now, locate the same sign and degree in your personal Natal chart and make a note of the house this degree falls in. The statement that corresponds with this house becomes your third statement. Go back to the Cosmic Check-In page and circle the three statements from the charts and read what you wrote. This will give you an idea about what to expect from this moon phase on a personal level. There is a video class that shows you how to read your personal chart at www.BlueMoonAcademy.com, look for *How to Use the Moon Book*.

I Feel, I Produce, I _____ .

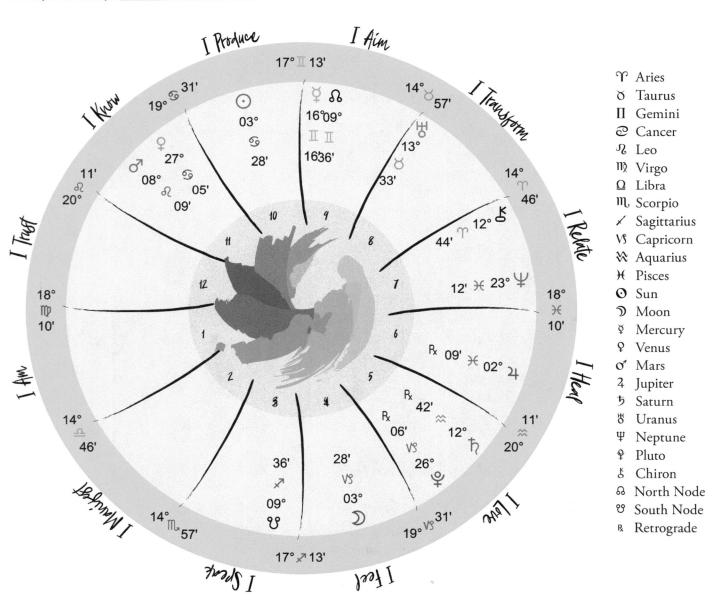

♈	Aries
♉	Taurus
♊	Gemini
♋	Cancer
♌	Leo
♍	Virgo
♎	Libra
♏	Scorpio
♐	Sagittarius
♑	Capricorn
♒	Aquarius
♓	Pisces
☉	Sun
☽	Moon
☿	Mercury
♀	Venus
♂	Mars
♃	Jupiter
♄	Saturn
♅	Uranus
♆	Neptune
♇	Pluto
⚷	Chiron
☊	North Node
☋	South Node
℞	Retrograde

Cosmic Check-In

Capricorn Full Moon
June 24th, 11:39 AM

Take a moment to write a brief phrase for each "I" statement. This activates all areas of your life for this creative cycle.

♑ I Produce

♒ I Know

♓ I Trust

♈ I Am

♉ I Manifest

♊ I Speak

♋ I Feel

♌ I Love

♍ I Heal

♎ I Relate

♏ I Transform

♐ I Aim

July

July 1st Jupiter retrograde in Pisces until the 17th of October

Jupiter is in the land of good fortune holding the space for all the wonders in life. When Jupiter goes retrograde, it is time to check in on what golden opportunities you might have missed over the last 12 years. Take a good look here, you may find hidden treasures waiting for you to wake up.

July 1st Saturn retrograde in Aquarius until the 10th of October

Time to use that brilliant mind to determine options to any situation. Inroads from the past may come up for review. Remember while reviewing, ask out loud, "What was the wisdom behind the event?" The more you use your mind to exchange experience for wisdom, the more Saturn will reward you.

July 1st Neptune retrograde in Pisces until December 1st

Expect to become keenly aware of other dimensions making themselves known to you. This is a good time to take a course on psychic development.

July 1st Pluto retrograde in Capricorn until 6th of October

You may notice survival issues coming forward to activate resistance to the transformation issues. A power statement to work with this transformation is, "I am willing to make NEW CHOICES that are beyond survival".

July 9th Venus conjunct Mars intercepted in Leo

Expect explosive energy perhaps from a feeling of confinement. This usually opens up a powerful magnetic vortex around making love. However, Leo is intercepting the passion and it becomes eclipsed by perfectionism on one end and too much attention on the past on the other. Time to remember to "make love not war!"

July 11th Mercury enters Pisces

This is a time when you might feel stifled. Sharing how you feel will not be easy. Let it be!

July 21st Venus enters Virgo

Expect to feel extra critical or analytical. Time to remember that complaining destroys creativity and causes fun to disappear. Begin to set boundaries and you might feel better!

July 22nd The Sun enters Leo

Time to shine! Let the light of the Sun guide you and all will be well!

July 27th Mercury enters Leo

Time to write love letters, a romance novel, or make a movie about the way you want to be loved.

July 28th Jupiter retrograde enters Aquarius

You may be setting the stage for a new standard for the future. Make sure you find the group/community to make that happen.

July 29th Mars enters Virgo

You've got the motives to strive for perfection. Do not sacrifice your well-being in a relentless instinct to be impeccable. That can lead to exhaustion. Image management can become a burden to yourself and others around you. Accept that you are perfect exactly as you are in all your magnificence!

Low Vitality July 7th-11th

Chaos is close, stay in your own boundaries. Particularly on the 9th through 11th beware of your language and speak your truth with love to avoid unneeded endings and misunderstandings.

Super Sensitivity July 20th and 21st

Watch out for a stream of consciousness pouring down from the galaxy. Watch it. Don't react to it.

SUNDAY	MONDAY	TUESDAY	WEDNESDAY	THURSDAY	FRIDAY	SATURDAY
				1 ♃♄♆♇℞ 10. Look to the future.	2 ♃♄♆♇℞ ☽ V/C 9:14 PM 11. Use your magic.	3 ♃♄♆♇℞ ☽→♉ 5:28 AM 3. Have a game night with friends.
4 ♃♄♆♇℞ **Independence Day** 4. Common sense says use sunblock.	5 ♃♄♆♇℞ ☽ V/C 9:56 AM ☽→♊ 6:24 PM 5. Go for an early morning walk.	6 ♃♄♆♇℞ 6. Create and enjoy a romantic dinner.	7 ♃♄♆♇℞▼ ☽ V/C 9:19 PM 7. Energy follows thought, use it well.	8 ♃♄♆♇℞▼ ☽→♋ 6:51 AM 8. Buy a lottery ticket.	9 ♃♄♆♇℞▼ ● 18° ♋ 02' 6:17 PM 9. Donate to service organizations.	10 ♃♄♆♇℞▼ ☽ V/C 9:09 AM ☽→♌ 5:21 PM 10. Be the leader you know you are.
11 ♃♄♆♇℞▼ ☿→♓ 1:35 PM 11. Act on your intuition.	12 ♃♄♆♇℞ ☽ V/C 5:28 AM 3. Make your day playful and happy.	13 ♃♄♆♇℞ ☽→♍ 1:31 AM 4. Pick a drawer, organize it.	14 ♃♄♆♇℞ ☽ V/C 11:46 PM 5. Relax and enjoy the ride.	15 ♃♄♆♇℞ ☽→♎ 7:31 AM 6. Love opens your heart.	16 ♃♄♆♇℞ 7. Take on a research project.	17 ♃♄♆♇℞ ☽ V/C 4:03 AM ☽→♏ 11:39 AM 8. Be willing to accept success.
18 ♃♄♆♇℞ 9. Loving service is a gift.	19 ♃♄♆♇℞ ☽ V/C 9:30 AM ☽→♐ 2:07 PM 10. Allow a new beginning to flourish.	20 ♃♄♆♇℞▲ 11. Accept that you are powerful.	21 ♃♄♆♇℞▲ ☽ V/C 3:25 PM ☽→♑ 3:37 PM ♀→♍ 5:36 PM 3. Be delighted by a child's creativity.	22 ♃♄♆♇℞ ☉→♌ 7:26 AM 4. Plant your feet on the Earth today.	23 ♃♄♆♇℞ ☽ V/C 9:34 AM ☽→♒ 5:13 PM ○ 1° ♒ 26' 7:37 PM 5. Expect a shift in mental awareness.	24 ♃♄♆♇℞ 6. Re-evaluate your diet.
25 ♃♄♆♇℞ ☽ V/C 4:13 PM ☽→♓ 8:29 PM 7. Learn a new technology.	26 ♃♄♆♇℞ 8. Let prosperity become you.	27 ♃♄♆♇℞ ☿→♌ 6:11 PM ☽ V/C 6:12 PM 9. Keep your boundaries clear.	28 ♃♄♆♇℞ ☽→♈ 2:58 AM ♃℞→♒ 4:48 PM 10. The future is now.	29 ♃♄♆♇℞ ♂→♍ 1:32 PM 11. Live your truth.	30 ♃♄♆♇℞ ☽ V/C 12:37 PM ☽→♉ 1:08 PM 3. Imagination creates breakthroughs.	31 ♃♄♆♇℞ 4. Need stability? Make a list.

♈ Aries	♍ Virgo	♒ Aquarius	♀ Venus	♆ Neptune	V/C Void-of-Course	2. Balance	7. Learning
♉ Taurus	♎ Libra	♓ Pisces	♂ Mars	♇ Pluto	℞ Retrograde	3. Fun	8. Money
♊ Gemini	♏ Scorpio	☉ Sun	♃ Jupiter	→ Enters	SD Stationary Direct	4. Structure	9. Spirituality
♋ Cancer	♐ Sagittarius	☽ Moon	♄ Saturn	● New Moon	▲ Super Sensitivity	5. Action	10. Visionary
♌ Leo	♑ Capricorn	☿ Mercury	♅ Uranus	○ Full Moon	▼ Low Vitality	6. Love	11. Completion

New Moon in Cancer

July 9th, 6:17 PM

When the Sun is in Cancer

It is now time to build our structure and foundation. Cancer holds the wisdom of the Great Cosmic Architect. Her statement is, "I build a lighted house and therein I dwell." The key is to use the materials of light, love, and wisdom to build your house and become the creator of form. Look within to see what lights your home and your body. Also check security systems, early environmental training, and mother/child relationships to see what materials you are using to build the structure for your life. Use this creating moon to build the structure you want.

Cancer Goddess

Hestia awakens your awareness to your surroundings. Take a good look around at your physical home and work areas. The Goddess of home and hearth arrives this moon to help you feather your nest, to bring comfort and peace to the places where you live and work. She can help sweep away clutter, catch your eye with a pleasing painting or photograph to enhance your space. Let her nurture you with her sense of beauty and order. Allow her to guide you in designing your altar, a meditation space, or a quiet hideaway protected from interruption. Ask her to put you at ease in your new yoga room or artist studio. Once at ease, your creativity will flow.

Hestia's home fires burned in everyone's homes, not just in temples. She was a practical and personal goddess, protecting the flame of love that was the center of every home. She received the first offering at every sacrifice in the home. Her sacred flame was the center of every city, the prytaneum, the public hearth. When a new city was established, Hestia's flame was carried there with honor. The centrality of her worship reminds you to put your taste, sensibilities, palate, and love first, and tranquility will abide in your home and in your community. The light of the flame of family love nourishes all.

Build Your Altar

Colors	Shades of gray, milky/creamy colors
Numerology	9 – Donate to service organizations
Tarot Card	Chariot – Victory through action
Gemstones	Pearl, moonstone, ruby
Plant Remedy	Shooting Star – The ability to move straight ahead
Fragrance	Peppermint – The essence of the Great Mother

Moon Notes

New Moon 18° Cancer 02'
New Moons are about opening new pathways for prosperity.

Element
Water – Taking the path of least resistance, going with the flow, secretive, sensual, glamorous, psychic, magnetic, escaping reality, a healer, an actor/actress, and creativity at its best.

Statement I Feel

Body Stomach

Mind Worry

Spirit Nurturing

7th House Moon I Relate/I Feel

Umbrella Energy
One-on-one relationships, defines your people attraction, and how you work in relationships with the people you attract.

Karmic Awakening
One Love/Group Love

Choice Points
Action   Charisma
Non-action   Manipulation

Sabian Symbol
Venetian Gondoliers Giving A Serenade.

Potential
Time to share knowledge.

Cancer Victories & Challenges

Say all of the statements in this section out loud. Then, underline the phrase that means the most to you. Use the phrase as your affirmation for manifesting throughout this moon phase.

Today I take advantage of my ability to take action and position myself for success. I clearly know that the road to success is before me, and all I need to do is move forward. I am aware that when I take action and move forward, the Universe fills in the dots. Whether I move left, right, or straight ahead doesn't matter—what matters is movement. Today, I release the indecisiveness that keeps me stuck. Today, I let go of vacillation that exhausts my mind. Today, I take my foot off of the brakes and find the gas pedal. I allow movement to occur, even if I don't know where I am going. When I take action, I trust that guideposts will appear. I am aware that action leads me to my new direction. So, today I know and GO! I remember that karma comes to the space of non-action, while success comes through action. Action brings me to my victory. Standing still leads to regret, resentment, and chaos. I am aware that action can be as simple as taking a walk on the beach, buying fresh flowers to add a new dimension to my home, or simply going to a new restaurant for lunch. I take action today to break up a crystallized pattern and, in so doing, my life begins to show me newfound awareness and light to guide me.

Cancer Homework

Cancers manifest best when catering, writing cookbooks, in marriage and family counseling, providing childcare, giving massage, or when engaged in genealogy, arts and crafts, architecture, and home-building.

During the Cancer new moon cycle, we are asked to turn light into form, and then turn it into beauty on four levels. Physically, we must feel nurtured and protected. Emotionally, we must set safe boundaries for the expression of our feelings. Mentally, we must release self-pity and embrace rightful thinking. Spiritually, we must hold the space for the infusion of light to shine inside all bodies on Earth.

Victory List

Acknowledge what you have overcome. Keep this list active during this moon cycle. Honoring victory allows you to accept success.

Tarot

Ask the question out loud, then draw a card. You may wish to draw it or paste a copy of it here. Then write down what you feel it might be telling you, in response to the question. Use the glossary in the appendix and record here anything about the card that captures your attention. You may wish to come back throughout the moon cycle to meditate or journal more on the card.

How is my heart supporting my manifesting?

Manifesting List

This or something better than this comes to me in an easy and pleasurable way, for the good of all concerned. Thank you, Universe!

Cancer Manifesting Ideas

Now is the time to focus on manifesting being a good mother, new ways to be a mom, nurturing and self-love, the ability to see joy, a clutter-free home, your dream home, and inner and outer security.

New Moon in Cancer

Your Personal Moon Experience

Fill in the Cosmic Check-In page. Then look up the Moon in the chart below. Take note of the "I" statement on the outside of the wheel where the Moon is located. This is the house the Moon is in, and the statement gives you the atmospheric energy, or the "umbrella energy" of this moon phase. This becomes the first statement to use in your mantra. Then, the "I" statement that corresponds with the astrological sign the Moon is in becomes the second statement (see *Moon Notes* for this moon phase). Now, locate the same sign and degree in your personal Natal chart and make a note of the house this degree falls in. The statement that corresponds with this house becomes your third statement. Go back to the Cosmic Check-In page and circle the three statements from the charts and read what you wrote. This will give you an idea about what to expect from this moon phase on a personal level. There is a video class that shows you how to read your personal chart at www.BlueMoonAcademy.com, look for *How to Use the Moon Book*.

I Relate, I Feel, I _____.

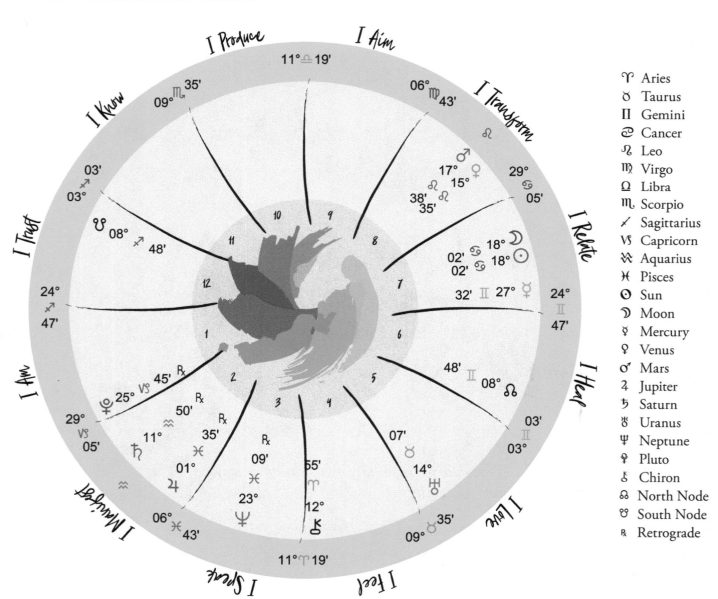

♈	Aries
♉	Taurus
♊	Gemini
♋	Cancer
♌	Leo
♍	Virgo
♎	Libra
♏	Scorpio
♐	Sagittarius
♑	Capricorn
♒	Aquarius
♓	Pisces
☉	Sun
☽	Moon
☿	Mercury
♀	Venus
♂	Mars
♃	Jupiter
♄	Saturn
♅	Uranus
♆	Neptune
♇	Pluto
⚷	Chiron
☊	North Node
☋	South Node
℞	Retrograde

Cosmic Check-In

Cancer New Moon
July 9th, 6:17 PM

Take a moment to write a brief phrase for each "I" statement. This activates all areas of your life for this creative cycle.

♋ I Feel

♌ I Love

♍ I Heal

♎ I Relate

♏ I Transform

♐ I Aim

♑ I Produce

♒ I Know

♓ I Trust

♈ I Am

♉ I Manifest

♊ I Speak

Full Moon in Aquarius

July 23rd, 7:37 PM

When the Sun is Opposite the Moon

Full moons are always in opposition to the Sun. This creates a feeling of tension between where you want to shine and how your feelings are flowing on a sensory level about the Sun's directive. The two forces seem like they are working against each other, yet they are on the same team displaying different techniques to obtain the same mission. The Aquarian/Leo polarity creates tension between the quest for group interaction and the recognition of self.

Aquarius Goddess

This Aquarius moon is full to the brim. A year from the height of 2020's social protests, Aquarius will not be satisfied until the old lifeless forms have been disintegrated and composted, and the balanced energy restored. Today call forth Gula, the water-bearer, ancient Sumerian goddess who was the irrigator, the one who ensured that the fields were sufficiently fed by the power of rain and floods into a state of abundant fertility. Stories say she watered the tree that formed the axis of the world and kept energies in balance. Star card in the tarot deck illustrates Gula's power. A woman stands balanced, one foot on the land, and the other in the water. She has jugs in both hands and pours water on both the land and into the pond. Symbolically, what pours forth is life-force energy, the essence of the air sign Aquarius. Gula's urns brought forth a sacred alchemy of transmutation. One amber jar held a shimmering liquid or light of purity, and she poured it into the other jar she held, an earthenware jar full of dark and muddy water. As the substances mixed, the dark muddy waters boiled and churned. Gradually the contents of both containers were transmuted into the same shimmering liquid light, as the purification process unified the higher and lower substances. Your body may feel the need for purification. Step into an Epsom salt bath and ask Gula to remove the negative and restore your natural physical energetic balance.

Build Your Altar

Colors	Electric colors, neon, multi-colors, pearl white
Numerology	5 – Expect a shift in mental awareness
Tarot Card	The Star – Follow your light, it knows where to go
Gemstones	Aquamarine, amethyst, opal
Plant remedy	Queen of the Night Cactus – Ability to see in the dark
Fragrance	Myrrh – Healing the nervous system

Moon Notes

Full Moon 1° Aquarius 26'
Full Moons are about moving beyond blocks and setting yourself free.

Element
Air – The breath of life that allows the mind to achieve new insights and fresh perspectives, abstract dreaming, freedom from attachments, codes of intelligence, and academic applications.

Statement I Know

Body Ankles

Mind Genius

Spirit Innovation

1st House Moon I Am/I Know

Umbrella Energy
Your outer appearance, the way you present yourself, the way you dress, the way you enter a room, and what you leave behind when you leave the room.

Karmic Awakening
One Love/Group Love

Choice Points
Action   Sudden Illumination
Non-action   Vulnerability

Sabian Symbol
A Deserter From The Navy.

Potential
Leaving an old identity behind.

Clearing the Slate

Sixty hours before the full moon negative traits connected to the astro-sign might become activated to trigger what needs to be released during the full moon phase. You may notice yourself becoming stubborn, escaping reality by living in the future, and the need to be rebellious if you feel frenzied or chaotic. Make a list, look in the mirror, and for each negative trait, tell yourself *I am sorry, I forgive you, thank you for your awareness,* and *I love you.* Now is the time to start doing your Sky Power Yoga poses so your physiology can feel supported during this moon phase. The poses and the teaching are available on BlueMoonAcademy.com. Enjoy!

Aquarius Victories & Challenges

Say all of the statements in this section out loud. Then, underline the phrase that means the most to you. Use the phrase as your affirmation for releasing throughout this moon phase.

Today my true potential can be realized. All I have to do is take a risk and know that my faith is in operation. My future is very bright and offers me a promise of things to come. Today is a day of destiny. I have chosen this day to determine a DESTINY PROMISE I MADE TO MYSELF BEFORE I CAME INTO THIS LIFE. All that is required of me is to move out of my comfort zone and take a risk. I am aware that faith cannot be determined without risk. I take the risk to move into the next space of creation in my life. I release fear and move into faith, knowing full well that my logic and reason are part of the fear that keeps me stuck.

I am reminded that the kingdom of heaven is open to the child. I find the child within me today to embrace what life has for me with open arms and a spirit of adventure. I know my true potential lives inside my magical child and she/he is willing to play and go for the gusto. I am here in this life to fulfill my promise to experience life to the fullest and to release the fear of judgment that has hounded me and kept me from playing full-out. I remember that when I experience, I gather a knowledge base within my Soul and keep my agreement with myself and the Universe. I connect to my super-consciousness and take on the bigger view of my life and all that it has to offer me when I risk reason and take a leap of faith. I know in the depth of my awareness that, if I jump off the diving board, there will be water in the pool. I am willing to risk reason for an experience. Everything I ever wanted is one step outside my comfort zone. I go for the GUSTO today! I release my fear today and turn it into faith. I trust in the promise of things to come. I know my potential is realized today, and that all I have to do is say "YES!" to life!

Aquarius Homework

The Aquarius moon reminds us of our connection to solar fire (the heart of the Sun) also known as the Heart of the Cosmos. During this time, we get our vitality recharged and our potent power comes into play motivating the masses to receive more energy to transmute into the new world. Voice all that you know to be true to the point of self-realization where your authentic purpose can be revealed to you. This is the moment where you have released all that has kept you from your true sense of freedom. Remember to replenish all the electrolytes in your system.

Gratitude List

Keep this list active throughout the moon cycle. This will bring you to a level of completion so that a new cycle of opportunity can occur in your life. Be prepared for miracles!

Tarot

Ask the question out loud, then draw a card. You may wish to draw it or paste a copy of it here. Then write down what you feel it might be telling you, in response to the question. Use the glossary in the appendix and record here anything about the card that captures your attention. You may wish to come back throughout the moon cycle to meditate or journal more on the card.

How is my mind supporting my releasing?

Releasing List

Say this statement out loud three times before writing your list:

I am a free spiritual being and it is my desire to be free to think and to express myself fully.

Freedom is mine when I live my truth!

Aquarius Releasing Ideas

Now is the time to activate a game change in my life, and give up resistance to authority figures, blocks to living in the moment, unnecessary rebellion, non-productive frenzy and fantasy, the need to be spontaneous, and people who aren't team players.

Full Moon in Aquarius

Your Personal Moon Experience

Fill in the Cosmic Check-In page. Then look up the Moon in the chart below. Take note of the "I" statement on the outside of the wheel where the Moon is located. This is the house the Moon is in, and the statement gives you the atmospheric energy, or the "umbrella energy" of this moon phase. This becomes the first statement to use in your mantra. Then, the "I" statement that corresponds with the astrological sign the Moon is in becomes the second statement (see *Moon Notes* for this moon phase). Now, locate the same sign and degree in your personal Natal chart and make a note of the house this degree falls in. The statement that corresponds with this house becomes your third statement. Go back to the Cosmic Check-In page and circle the three statements from the charts and read what you wrote. This will give you an idea about what to expect from this moon phase on a personal level. There is a video class that shows you how to read your personal chart at www.BlueMoonAcademy.com, look for *How to Use the Moon Book*.

I Am, I Know, I _____ .

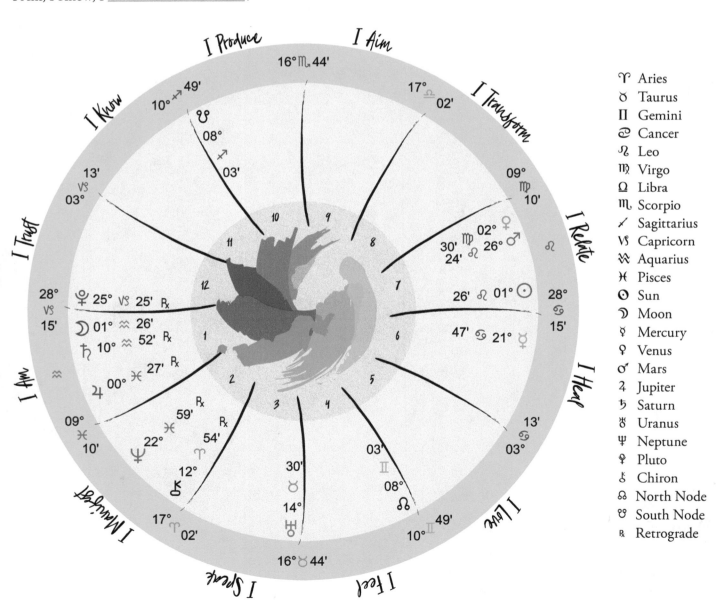

♈	Aries
♉	Taurus
♊	Gemini
♋	Cancer
♌	Leo
♍	Virgo
♎	Libra
♏	Scorpio
♐	Sagittarius
♑	Capricorn
♒	Aquarius
♓	Pisces
☉	Sun
☽	Moon
☿	Mercury
♀	Venus
♂	Mars
♃	Jupiter
♄	Saturn
♅	Uranus
♆	Neptune
♀	Pluto
⚷	Chiron
☊	North Node
☋	South Node
℞	Retrograde

Cosmic Check-In

Aquarius Full Moon
July 23rd, 7:37 PM

Take a moment to write a brief phrase for each "I" statement. This activates all areas of your life for this creative cycle.

♒ I Know

♓ I Trust

♈ I Am

♉ I Manifest

♊ I Speak

♋ I Feel

♌ I Love

♍ I Heal

♎ I Relate

♏ I Transform

♐ I Aim

♑ I Produce

August

August 1st Jupiter retrograde in Pisces until the 17th of October

Time to look into the year 2008 to see what was up around love, health, and home. See if there are any unresolved issues from that time. Making new choices around these issues may bring you some good fortune.

August 1st Saturn retrograde in Aquarius until the 10th of October

Look to see where you might have been misguided in your zeal to be of service. Time to check in with authorities to determine the integrity of the group involved. You may discover it does not match your intention. Time to make a change to a new group.

August 1st Neptune retrograde in Pisces until December 1st

Expect to be aware of unworldly dreams or visions. Smoke and mirrors can come into play here. Remember what you may see is symbolic, not real. Time to take a class in psychic development.

August 1st Pluto retrograde in Capricorn until 6th of October

This is a time to collect old debt or pay off old debt. Use this time wisely and you might be surprised by an unexpected pay back. Enjoy!

August 11th Mercury moves into Virgo

Time to pay attention to your mind. Watch out for becoming too analytical as it could exhaust you! Focus on your true power here that is raising the standard of excellence and all will be well!

August 15th Venus moves into Libra

Time to rest in the arms of your true love. This is a very special connection. Let it bring you to a space of balance.

August 19th Uranus goes retrograde in Taurus until next year

Calm, slow-moving, easy-going Taurus has been hit by an electrical current that has sent shock waves throughout the earth. The whole motivation has been to kick up enough speed so the earth can make the goal of the decade, to transform. This retrograde will go back, reset, and smooth out the shock waves to adjust to the new earth.

August 22nd Mars and Mercury are coupled in Virgo

This is a highly electric current exchange designed to widen pathways so that they hold larger energy fields.

August 22nd the Moon and Jupiter are coupled in Aquarius

Jupiter connects with the Moon to amplify the magnetic power of your receptivity so you can handle receiving more abundance.

August 22nd The Sun moves into Virgo

Time to shine the light into the small spaces so the light body advancement can manifest without expansion stress.

August 29th Mercury moves into Libra

At this time a questioning mind could diminish life experience by being too analytical. Take time to bask in the equation of relating rather than thinking.

Low Vitality August 3rd-4th and 30th-31st

Expect to be exhausted. Special care for the body is in order. Earth changes are very possible due to the energetic adjustments happening on the earth plane at this time.

Super Sensitivity August 16th-17th

The atmosphere is set up right now with tons of new knowledge for the Earth and her healing. Hold the space and keep your boundaries in place and all will be well!

SUNDAY	MONDAY	TUESDAY	WEDNESDAY	THURSDAY	FRIDAY	SATURDAY
1 ♃♄♆♇℞ 5. An adventure awaits you.	**2** ♃♄♆♇℞ ☽ V/C 12:40 AM ☽→♊ 1:47 AM 6. Does your home need attention?	**3** ♃♄♆♇℞▼ 7. Seek out the wisdom of an elder.	**4** ♃♄♆♇℞▼ ☽ V/C 12:37 PM ☽→♋ 2:17 PM 8. It's your choice to manifest or not.	**5** ♃♄♆♇℞ 9. All truths feed upon themselves.	**6** ♃♄♆♇℞ ☽ V/C 3:11 PM 10. You create your future.	**7** ♃♄♆♇℞ ☽→♌ 12:31 AM 11. Define your kingdom.
8 ♃♄♆♇℞ ● 16° ♌ 14' 6:51 AM 4. Be a stable influence today.	**9** ♃♄♆♇℞ ☽ V/C 5:22 AM ☽→♍ 7:55 AM 5. Go with the flow.	**10** ♃♄♆♇℞ 6. Love heals many.	**11** ♃♄♆♇℞ ☽ V/C 4:21 AM ☽→♎ 1:08 PM ☿→♍ 2:56 PM 7. A day for 'discernment in action.'	**12** ♃♄♆♇℞ 8. Ambition leads to a goal.	**13** ♃♄♆♇℞ ☽ V/C 1:38 PM ☽→♏ 5:01 PM 9. Meditate on world harmony.	**14** ♃♄♆♇℞ 10. Transform an idea into action.
15 ♃♄♆♇℞ ☽ V/C 8:04 PM ☽→♐ 8:12 PM ♀→♎ 9:26 PM 11. Use your intuition today.	**16** ♃♄♆♇℞▲ 3. Create art with what you have.	**17** ♃♄♆♇℞▲ ☽ V/C 6:42 PM ☽→♑ 10:58 PM 4. Accept the plan.	**18** ♃♄♆♇℞ 5. Plan a travel adventure.	**19** ♃♄♅♆♇℞ ☽ V/C 4:59 PM ♅℞ 14° ♉ 48' 6:40 PM 6. Spend time with your family.	**20** ♃♄♅♆♇℞ ☽→♒ 1:48 AM 7. Problem solving is easier today.	**21** ♃♄♅♆♇℞ 8. Manifesting is effortless today.
22 ♃♄♅♆♇℞ ☽ V/C 5:01 AM ○ 29° ♒ 37' 5:02 AM ☽→♓ 5:42 AM ☉→♍ 2:35 PM 9. Breathe in wisdom, breathe out grace.	**23** ♃♄♅♆♇℞ 10. Lead with an innovative vision.	**24** ♃♄♅♆♇℞ ☽ V/C 2:12 AM ☽→♈ 11:57 AM 11. The universe is yours, own it.	**25** ♃♄♅♆♇℞ 3. Optimism creates ease and joy.	**26** ♃♄♅♆♇℞ ☽ V/C 2:14 PM ☽→♉ 9:27 PM 4. What structure needs a change?	**27** ♃♄♅♆♇℞ 5. Grab a friend and go for a walk.	**28** ♃♄♅♆♇℞ 6. Live love every day.
29 ♃♄♅♆♇℞ ☽ V/C 7:58 AM ☽→♊ 9:42 PM ☿→♎ 10:10 PM 7. Peace expands knowledge.	**30** ♃♄♅♆♇℞▼ 8. Diligence is success in action.	**31** ♃♄♅♆♇℞▼ ☽ V/C 1:48 PM ☽→♋ 10:26 PM 9. Generosity multiplies.				

♈ Aries	♍ Virgo	♒ Aquarius	♀ Venus	♆ Neptune	V/C Void-of-Course	2. Balance	7. Learning
♉ Taurus	♎ Libra	♓ Pisces	♂ Mars	♇ Pluto	℞ Retrograde	3. Fun	8. Money
♊ Gemini	♏ Scorpio	☉ Sun	♃ Jupiter	→ Enters	SD Stationary Direct	4. Structure	9. Spirituality
♋ Cancer	♐ Sagittarius	☽ Moon	♄ Saturn	● New Moon	▲ Super Sensitivity	5. Action	10. Visionary
♌ Leo	♑ Capricorn	☿ Mercury	♅ Uranus	○ Full Moon	▼ Low Vitality	6. Love	11. Completion

New Moon in Leo

August 8th, 6:51 AM

When the Sun is in Leo

This is the time when you feel the power from the Sun, the heart of the Cosmos. Leo has a direct relationship with the Sun's heart. The Sun rules your identity. Now is the time to shine and stand tall in the center of your life. Allow yourself to feel the power of your individual conscious Self. When you align with the power of the Sun, you become radiant. This radiance gives you the power to transmit energy into life. Personal fulfillment becomes a reality when you align your will with love. Remember to live love every day!

Leo Goddess

The Shinto Sun Goddess of Japan, Amaterasu's name means "shining in heaven" and all Japanese emperors are said to be her descendants. Depicted with shining rays of sunlight emanating from her head, she is central to Japanese spiritual life, as the source of divine justice, order, and purity. She once retreated to a cave and with her went the warmth of the sun, hidden from humankind. She became curious as to how the other gods could dance and sing and be happy in a world full of darkness. She was told that outside the cave there was a more luminous deity than she, but when she looked out, she saw her own reflection in a sacred mirror, a cock crowed to signal the dawn, and she was drawn out of the cave, lighting the world once more.

We all have times when we lose the sense of our luminous selves. Find yourself a friend to pair off. Sit opposite each other with a candle in between. Taking turns, be the sacred mirror for the person sitting across from you and tell them what you see. Allow the first person to speak for two minutes while the other listens, without interrupting, belittling or shrugging off anything that is said. Then switch places. To end, put a hand on each other's power chakras, midway between the heart and the belly button, and exchange your renewed light through your eyes. Allow Amaterasu to draw you out of your cave to shine your light in a world filled with darkness.

Build Your Altar

Colors   Royal purple, royal blue, orange

Numerology   4 – Be a stable influence today

Tarot Card   Sun – Accept abundance and the ability to have it all

Gemstones   Peridot, emerald, amber

Plant Remedy Sunflower – Standing tall in the center of your garden

Fragrance   Jasmine – Remembering your Soul's original intention

Moon Notes

New Moon   16° Leo 14'
New Moons are about opening new pathways for prosperity.

Element
Fire – Igniting, dissolving, accelerating, cleansing, advancing awareness, impatience, leadership, passion, and vitality.

Statement   I Love

Body   Heart and Spinal Cord

Mind   Self-confidence

Spirit   Generosity

12th House Moon   I Trust/I Love

Umbrella Energy
Determines how you deal with your karma, and what you will experience in order to attain mastery to complete your karma. The way you connect to the Divine.

Choice Points
Action   Community Contribution
Non-action   Not Good Enough

Sabian Symbol
The Storm Ended, All Nature Rejoices In Brilliant Sunshine.

Potential
Celebrate this new beginning!

Leo Victories & Challenges

Say all of the statements in this section out loud. Then, underline the phrase that means the most to you. Use the phrase as your affirmation for manifesting throughout this moon phase.

Today, I am at the center of bliss, happiness, abundance, and total celebration. It is my time to shine and feel the power of my true self blasting the Universe, the entire planet, and all of life with the light of my awareness. There is nothing that can stop me today, because I am free to be me. When I am free to be me, I can stand naked in the daylight and have nothing to hide. I truly know that all of life loves me and I love all of life. I feel the radiance and vibration of my being activating me with aliveness, vitality, and charisma. I know that I can make a difference because I celebrate life by infusing, sparking, and igniting matter with light. I am open and ready to embrace all that comes to me with joy. I say "YES!" to all opportunities today; knowing that today is my day. I am in the flow of abundance and I let abundance flow through me.

The child within me is open and ready to play full out; there is not a cloud in the sky today that can eclipse me or place a shadow on me and keep me from my true level of power. I am aware that the child state of being within me simply says yes to action and action is power. When I take action today, my possibilities are endless because they are generated from my true self and motivated by happiness, joy, and freedom. The child within me is able to play full out because I have birthed myself beyond my old perception of blocks. I know that in taking this true power, to be motivated by happiness, pathways on all levels and in all dimensions can open to the empowerment of joy. Empowerment is mine today because I am shining from within myself and I know my deepest self is connected to the source. Empowerment occurs when I live from the inside out. Today, I wave the banner of my being from within, feel the glow, and go.

Leo Homework

Leos manifest best through fashion and jewelry design, glamour, politics, super-modeling, movie stardom, child advocacy, fundraising, toy and game design, image consulting, authoring children's books, sales, and cardiology.

Leo gets you closer to your essential self, reminding you of your Soul's original intention. You become ready to receive the benefits of reflective light and radiating light at the same time, so that you can see your personality and your Soul connecting to love which constitutes a new level of fulfillment. Expect purification, transmutation, communication, and mastery to be part of your personal experience.

Victory List

Acknowledge what you have overcome. Keep this list active during this moon cycle.
Honoring victory allows you to accept success.

Tarot

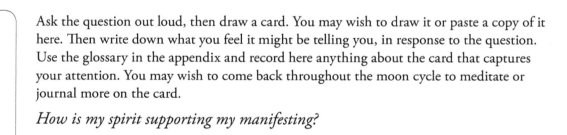

Ask the question out loud, then draw a card. You may wish to draw it or paste a copy of it here. Then write down what you feel it might be telling you, in response to the question. Use the glossary in the appendix and record here anything about the card that captures your attention. You may wish to come back throughout the moon cycle to meditate or journal more on the card.

How is my spirit supporting my manifesting?

Manifesting List

This or something better than this comes to me in an easy and pleasurable way, for the good of all concerned. Thank you, Universe!

Leo Manifesting Ideas

Now is the time to focus on manifesting new love or new ways of loving, new creative ways of expressing myself, bonding with those I love, quality time with those I love, knowledge of my Soul's intention, fun with my children, being a bright beaming light, and connecting to the hearts of humanity.

New Moon in Leo

Your Personal Moon Experience

Fill in the Cosmic Check-In page. Then look up the Moon in the chart below. Take note of the "I" statement on the outside of the wheel where the Moon is located. This is the house the Moon is in, and the statement gives you the atmospheric energy, or the "umbrella energy" of this moon phase. This becomes the first statement to use in your mantra. Then, the "I" statement that corresponds with the astrological sign the Moon is in becomes the second statement (see *Moon Notes* for this moon phase). Now, locate the same sign and degree in your personal Natal chart and make a note of the house this degree falls in. The statement that corresponds with this house becomes your third statement. Go back to the Cosmic Check-In page and circle the three statements from the charts and read what you wrote. This will give you an idea about what to expect from this moon phase on a personal level. There is a video class that shows you how to read your personal chart at www.BlueMoonAcademy.com, look for *How to Use the Moon Book*.

I Trust, I Love, I _____ .

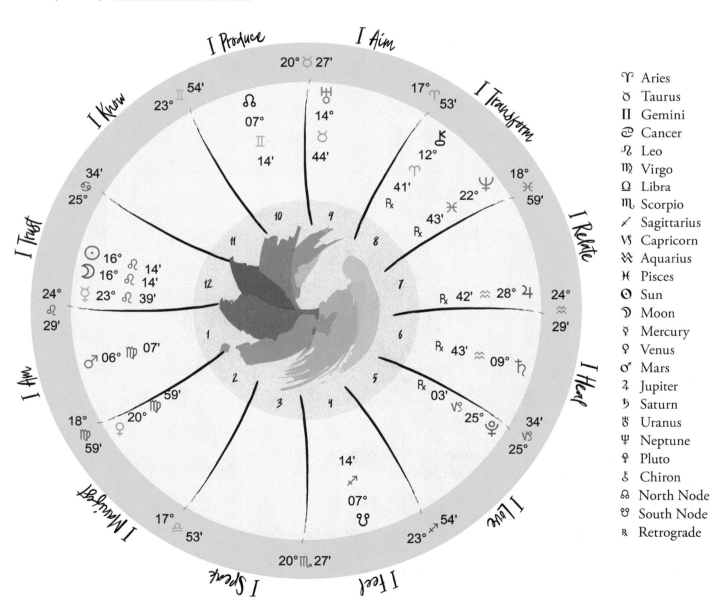

♈	Aries
♉	Taurus
♊	Gemini
♋	Cancer
♌	Leo
♍	Virgo
♎	Libra
♏	Scorpio
♐	Sagittarius
♑	Capricorn
♒	Aquarius
♓	Pisces
☉	Sun
☽	Moon
☿	Mercury
♀	Venus
♂	Mars
♃	Jupiter
♄	Saturn
♅	Uranus
♆	Neptune
♇	Pluto
⚷	Chiron
☊	North Node
☋	South Node
℞	Retrograde

Cosmic Check-In

Leo New Moon
August 8th, 6:51 AM

Take a moment to write a brief phrase for each "I" statement. This activates all areas of your life for this creative cycle.

♌ I Love

♍ I Heal

♎ I Relate

♏ I Transform

♐ I Aim

♑ I Produce

♒ I Know

♓ I Trust

♈ I Am

♉ I Manifest

♊ I Speak

♋ I Feel

Full Moon in Aquarius

August 22nd, 5:02 AM

When the Sun is Opposite the Moon

Full moons are always in opposition to the Sun. This creates a feeling of tension between where you want to shine and how your feelings are flowing on a sensory level about the Sun's directive. The two forces seem like they are working against each other, yet they are on the same team displaying different techniques to obtain the same mission. The Aquarian/Leo polarity creates tension between the quest for group interaction and the recognition of self.

Aquarius Goddess

Atabey, the Taino Goddess of fresh water and fertility; earth spirit of lakes, streams and tidal waters; rises out of the pool of primal matter. One side of Atabey is maternal, watching over mothers in childbirth and bringing all the spirit of love and peace; while the other side is the wild mother nature of earthquakes, volcanoes and tempestuous storms--chaos embodied. The Taino word "hurakan" survived from the pre-Columbian times in the Caribbean, as our word "hurricane." Atabey's likeness was very much reminiscent of a Sheila-na-gig, a naked woman in childbearing squat. But just as childbirth has its storm of pain, screaming and uncertainty during labor and delivery, a mother perseveres and the spirit of love awaits her on the other side of the storm. The purification process is not for the faint of heart. In a flood of unwelcome change--you are tossed and torn from all that is familiar. But that sort of radical clearing can also bring a renewed appreciation for the most important things in life, which are rarely 'things' at all, but relationships with loved ones from which comes one's sense of home. What storms have invaded your personal spaces and family dynamics? When the root chakra is challenged, deep survival issues can surface. Find some quiet time to reflect and journal on how the past year has transformed you and what lessons you may have learned.

Build Your Altar

Colors	Electric colors, neon, multi-colors, pearl white
Numerology	9 – Breathe in wisdom, breathe out grace
Tarot Card	The Star – Follow your light, it knows where to go
Gemstones	Aquamarine, amethyst, opal
Plant remedy	Queen of the Night Cactus – Ability to see in the dark
Fragrance	Myrrh – Healing the nervous system

Moon Notes

Full Moon 29° Aquarius 37'
Full Moons are about moving beyond blocks and setting yourself free.

Element
Air – The breath of life that allows the mind to achieve new insights and fresh perspectives, abstract dreaming, freedom from attachments, codes of intelligence, and academic applications.

Statement I Know

Body Ankles

Mind Genius

Spirit Innovation

7th House Moon I Relate/I Know

Umbrella Energy
One-on-one relationships, defines your people attraction, and how you work in relationships with the people you attract.

Choice Points
Action   Ancient Wonders
Non-action   Scapegoating

Sabian Symbol
Deeply Rooted In The Past Of A Very Ancient Culture, A Spiritual Brotherhood In Which Many Individual Minds Are Merged Into The Glowing Light Of A Unanimous Consciousness Is Revealed To One Who Has Emerged Successfully From His Metamorphosis.

Potential
Transformation at last.

Clearing the Slate

Sixty hours before the full moon negative traits connected to the astro-sign might become activated to trigger what needs to be released during the full moon phase. You may notice yourself becoming stubborn, escaping reality by living in the future, and the need to be rebellious if you feel frenzied or chaotic. Make a list, look in the mirror, and for each negative trait, tell yourself *I am sorry, I forgive you, thank you for your awareness,* and *I love you.* Now is the time to start doing your Sky Power Yoga poses so your physiology can feel supported during this moon phase. The poses and the teaching are available on BlueMoonAcademy.com. Enjoy!

Aquarius Victories & Challenges

Say all of the statements in this section out loud. Then, underline the phrase that means the most to you. Use the phrase as your affirmation for releasing throughout this moon phase.

Today my true potential can be realized. All I have to do is take a risk and know that my faith is in operation. My future is very bright and offers me a promise of things to come. Today is a day of destiny. I have chosen this day to determine a DESTINY PROMISE I MADE TO MYSELF BEFORE I CAME INTO THIS LIFE. All that is required of me is to move out of my comfort zone and take a risk. I am aware that faith cannot be determined without risk. I take the risk to move into the next space of creation in my life. I release fear and move into faith, knowing full well that my logic and reason are part of the fear that keeps me stuck.

I am reminded that the kingdom of heaven is open to the child. I find the child within me today to embrace what life has for me with open arms and a spirit of adventure. I know my true potential lives inside my magical child and she/he is willing to play and go for the gusto. I am here in this life to fulfill my promise to experience life to the fullest and to release the fear of judgment that has hounded me and kept me from playing full-out. I remember that when I experience, I gather a knowledge base within my Soul and keep my agreement with myself and the Universe. I connect to my super-consciousness and take on the bigger view of my life and all that it has to offer me when I risk reason and take a leap of faith. I know in the depth of my awareness that, if I jump off the diving board, there will be water in the pool. I am willing to risk reason for an experience. Everything I ever wanted is one step outside my comfort zone. I go for the GUSTO today! I release my fear today and turn it into faith. I trust in the promise of things to come. I know my potential is realized today, and that all I have to do is say "YES!" to life!

Aquarius Homework

The Aquarius moon reminds us of our connection to solar fire (the heart of the Sun) also known as the Heart of the Cosmos. During this time, we get our vitality recharged and our potent power comes into play motivating the masses to receive more energy to transmute into the new world. Voice all that you know to be true to the point of self-realization where your authentic purpose can be revealed to you. This is the moment where you have released all that has kept you from your true sense of freedom. Remember to replenish all the electrolytes in your system.

Gratitude List

Keep this list active throughout the moon cycle. This will bring you to a level of completion so that a new cycle of opportunity can occur in your life. Be prepared for miracles!

Tarot

Ask the question out loud, then draw a card. You may wish to draw it or paste a copy of it here. Then write down what you feel it might be telling you, in response to the question. Use the glossary in the appendix and record here anything about the card that captures your attention. You may wish to come back throughout the moon cycle to meditate or journal more on the card.

How is my mind supporting my releasing?

Releasing List

Say this statement out loud three times before writing your list:

I am a free spiritual being and it is my desire to be free to think and to express myself fully.

Freedom is mine when I live my truth!

Aquarius Releasing Ideas

Now is the time to activate a game change in my life, and give up resistance to authority figures, blocks to living in the moment, unnecessary rebellion, non-productive frenzy and fantasy, the need to be spontaneous, and people who aren't team players.

Full Moon in Aquarius

Your Personal Moon Experience

Fill in the Cosmic Check-In page. Then look up the Moon in the chart below. Take note of the "I" statement on the outside of the wheel where the Moon is located. This is the house the Moon is in, and the statement gives you the atmospheric energy, or the "umbrella energy" of this moon phase. This becomes the first statement to use in your mantra. Then, the "I" statement that corresponds with the astrological sign the Moon is in becomes the second statement (see *Moon Notes* for this moon phase). Now, locate the same sign and degree in your personal Natal chart and make a note of the house this degree falls in. The statement that corresponds with this house becomes your third statement. Go back to the Cosmic Check-In page and circle the three statements from the charts and read what you wrote. This will give you an idea about what to expect from this moon phase on a personal level. There is a video class that shows you how to read your personal chart at www.BlueMoonAcademy.com, look for *How to Use the Moon Book*.

I Relate, I Know, I _____.

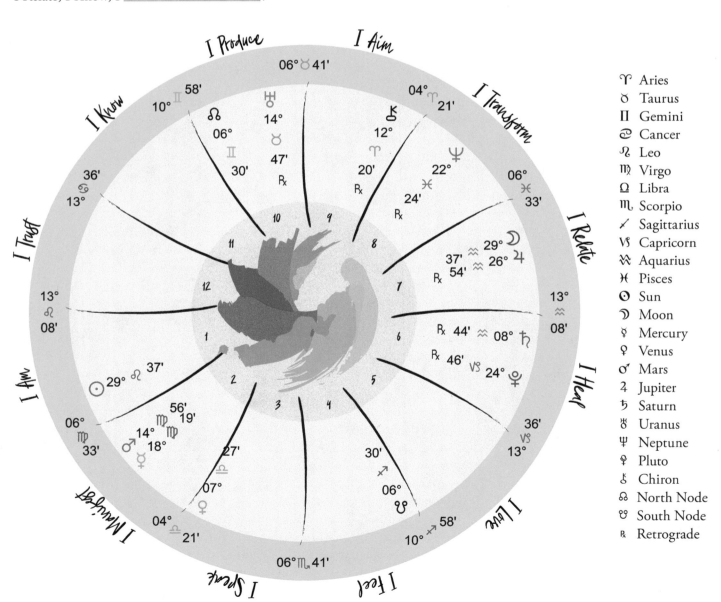

♈	Aries
♉	Taurus
♊	Gemini
♋	Cancer
♌	Leo
♍	Virgo
♎	Libra
♏	Scorpio
♐	Sagittarius
♑	Capricorn
♒	Aquarius
♓	Pisces
☉	Sun
☽	Moon
☿	Mercury
♀	Venus
♂	Mars
♃	Jupiter
♄	Saturn
♅	Uranus
♆	Neptune
♇	Pluto
⚷	Chiron
☊	North Node
☋	South Node
℞	Retrograde

Cosmic Check-In

Aquarius Full Moon
August 22nd, 5:02 AM

Take a moment to write a brief phrase for each "I" statement. This activates all areas of your life for this creative cycle.

♒ I Know

♓ I Trust

♈ I Am

♉ I Manifest

♊ I Speak

♋ I Feel

♌ I Love

♍ I Heal

♎ I Relate

♏ I Transform

♐ I Aim

♑ I Produce

September

September 1st Jupiter retrograde in Pisces until the 17th of October

You may feel motivated to be spiritually minded due to the retrograde. It's time to look for unfinished business for you in that area. For example, if you forgot to follow through on a project or let a promise go by the wayside.

September 1st Saturn retrograde in Aquarius until the 10th of October

This is a time to do a standard of excellence checkup. Where do you feel that your experience of life right now is not up to speed? Time to up the degree of your input and rearrange your life to determine good use of your energy. Maybe you are suffering from mental exhaustion because you are putting too much energy into image management.

September 1st Neptune retrograde in Pisces until December 1st

You could feel disappointed at this time of review if you discover too many dreams that didn't come true. This is a time to determine what to do; upgrade the dream and bring it back to real time or let it go and make room for new dreams to come forward.

September 1st Uranus retrograde in Taurus until next year

Uranus arrived in Taurus about a year ago after being in Aries for seven years. It arrived just in time so that Taurus could advance and be part of the future. During this retrograde, the earth may begin to realize that it was going to be left behind. So, we may feel some upgrades during this time in the form of earth changes.

September 1st Pluto retrograde in Capricorn until 6th of October

This is a time when review regarding survival issues can come into play. Use this time wisely to determine where survival issues are motivating your choices. Make amends with this and see how you can move beyond it. Time to make new choices!

September 10th Venus enters Scorpio

Expect great sex.

September 14th Mars enters Libra

Time to look for feminine/masculine balance. In relationships, keep your own boundaries clear.

September 20th Neptune retrograde conjunct the Moon in Virgo

This will be an emotional connection to your mother that needs healing or it will be an emotional connection within yourself providing motivation for being of service in the healing arts.

September 22nd the Sun enters Libra

This is when the sun shines on one-on-one relationships. The Autumn Equinox awakens our prosperity and abundance to harvest what we planted this year. Time to get your journal out and ask yourself, "What is the wisdom behind this event?", "Am I living for myself?", "Am I living for the community and forgetting myself?", "Am I lost in the identity of my relationship?", "Do I use family to not express myself fully?" Soul searching here is the best use of your time and the answers will set you free!

September 26th Mercury goes retrograde in Libra until October 18th

Watch out for the windshield wipers of the mind causing you to get exhausted. Remember if you can't make a decision in two minutes don't make one.

Super Sensitivity September 13th and 14th

The chaotic atmosphere is overloaded at this time. Remember it is universal, not personal. If you try to connect, you will find yourself in a frenzy. Keep your mental boundaries intact.

Low Vitality September 27th-28th

Take these days off resting or watching a TV marathon. Avoid pushing the envelope at this time. Nurture yourself.

SUNDAY	MONDAY	TUESDAY	WEDNESDAY	THURSDAY	FRIDAY	SATURDAY
			1 ♃♄♅♆♇℞ 10. Act on your ideas.	2 ♃♄♅♆♇℞ ☽ V/C 10:37 PM 11. Accept divine guidance.	3 ♃♄♅♆♇℞ ☽→♌ 8:59 AM 3. Gather friends for a fun day.	4 ♃♄♅♆♇℞ 4. What needs to be put in order?
5 ♃♄♅♆♇℞ ☽ V/C 7:21 AM 5. Take action today.	6 ♃♄♅♆♇℞ **Labor Day** **Rosh Hashanah Begins at Sunset** ☽→♍ 4:06 PM ● 14° ♍ 38' 5:52 PM 6. Is your body asking for attention?	7 ♃♄♅♆♇℞ ☽ V/C 12:23 PM ☽→♎ 8:21 PM 7. Keep the faith, trust your knowing.	8 ♃♄♅♆♇℞ **Rosh Hashanah Ends at Nightfall** 8. Yay! Celebrate your success today.	9 ♃♄♅♆♇℞ ☽ V/C 9:47 PM ☽→♏ 11:05 PM 9. Pray for balance and harmony.	10 ♃♄♅♆♇℞ ♀→♏ 1:39 PM 10. Give direction to your intention.	11 ♃♄♅♆♇℞ ☽ V/C 10:32 PM 11. All is in divine right order.
12 ♃♄♅♆♇℞ ☽→♐ 1:34 AM 3. Are you ready to create?	13 ♃♄♅♆♇℞▲ 4. Order solves many problems.	14 ♃♄♅♆♇℞▲ ☽ V/C 3:57 AM ☽→♑ 4:35 AM ♂→♎ 5:14 PM 5. Change is supported today.	15 ♃♄♅♆♇℞ **Yom Kippur Begins at Sunset** ☽ V/C 10:39 PM 6. Share the love.	16 ♃♄♅♆♇℞ **Yom Kippur Ends at Nightfall** ☽→♒ 8:22 AM 7. Your mental brilliance is activated.	17 ♃♄♅♆♇℞ 8. Timing is everything.	18 ♃♄♅♆♇℞ ☽ V/C 2:14 AM ☽→♓ 1:23 PM 9. We all want harmony.
19 ♃♄♅♆♇℞ 10. Be courageous, take the next step.	20 ♃♄♅♆♇℞ ☽ V/C 4:54 PM ○ 28° ♓ 14' 4:55 PM ☽→♈ 8:13 PM 11. Let truth resonate in your soul.	21 ♃♄♅♆♇℞ 3. Music helps creativity flow.	22 ♃♄♅♆♇℞ **Autumnal Equinox** ☉→♎ 12:21 PM ☽ V/C 7:04 PM 4. Trustworthiness is a virtue.	23 ♃♄♅♆♇℞ ☽→♉ 5:38 AM 5. Energy is speeding up, adjust.	24 ♃♄♅♆♇℞ 6. Hold harmony in all you do.	25 ♃♄♅♆♇℞ ☽ V/C 6:09 AM ☽→♊ 5:37 PM 7. Solutions are readily available.
26 ☿♃♄♅♆♇℞ ☿℞ 25° ♎ 28' 10:10 PM 8. Choose success.	27 ☿♃♄♅♆♇℞▼ ☽ V/C 9:18 PM 9. Every path is unique.	28 ☿♃♄♅♆♇℞▼ ☽→♋ 6:35 AM 10. Expect something new to begin.	29 ☿♃♄♅♆♇℞ 11. Let go and let God.	30 ☿♃♄♅♆♇℞ ☽ V/C 7:48 AM ☽→♌ 5:64 PM 3. Learn by watching children play.		

♈ Aries	♍ Virgo	♒ Aquarius	♀ Venus	♆ Neptune	V/C Void-of-Course	2. Balance	7. Learning
♉ Taurus	♎ Libra	♓ Pisces	♂ Mars	♇ Pluto	℞ Retrograde	3. Fun	8. Money
♊ Gemini	♏ Scorpio	☉ Sun	♃ Jupiter	→ Enters	S̶ Stationary Direct	4. Structure	9. Spirituality
♋ Cancer	♐ Sagittarius	☽ Moon	♄ Saturn	● New Moon	▲ Super Sensitivity	5. Action	10. Visionary
♌ Leo	♑ Capricorn	☿ Mercury	♅ Uranus	○ Full Moon	▼ Low Vitality	6. Love	11. Completion

New Moon in Virgo

September 6th, 5:52 PM

When the Sun is in Virgo

Virgo is called the "Womb of Time" in which the seeds of great value are planted, shielded, nourished, and revealed. It is the labor of Virgo that brings the Christ Principle into manifestation within individuals and humanity. This unification occurs when we feel the power within us to serve. When we serve, we give birth to Divinity. Virgo time is when we all have a chance to raise the standard of excellence in our lives and on the Earth. The Virgo intelligence stores and maintains light in a precise manner. Attention to detail is Virgo's great gift to life.

Virgo Goddess

Shala/Sala the Sumerian goddess of grain was synonymous with compassion, for the Sumerians believed a good harvest was an act of benevolence from the gods. A 10th century BC inscription praised Sala as "She who safeguards the life of the people." The constellation Virgo, called "The Furrow" by ancient Babylonians, represented Sala holding an ear of corn. Indeed, Spica, the brightest star of Virgo, was named for the Latin words for "spike" or "ear of corn." The ancients depended on Spica, a personification of Sala, as a calendar demarcation, for it disappeared in the west just after sunset at harvest time for wheat, and it reappeared in the east when wheat was ready to be threshed, about six weeks later. It alone tracked these agricultural events. Practical, simple, earthy, orderly – Virgo divinity in the details. That so many goddesses this year are earthy goddesses aligned with abundant harvests is no mistake. Sala, the compassionate provider/protector of the people, comes now to help restore order and constancy. 2020 was certainly a demarcation line for our generation – we will henceforth speak in terms of 'before' and 'after' 2020. What have you learned about yourself over the past year, as many lines were drawn in the sand? For some, demarcation came from the pandemic, for others, the social justice protests, and for others, the election or the death of Ruth Bader Ginsburg. Check in with your heart. How has order re-assembled in your life and world?

Build Your Altar

Colors	Earth tones, blue, green
Numerology	6 – Your body may be asking for attention
Tarot Card	The Hermit – Be willing to get off the mountain top and go be of service
Gemstones	Emerald, malachite, sapphire
Plant Remedy	Sagebrush – The ability to hold and store light
Fragrance	Lavender – Management and storage of energy

Moon Notes

New Moon 14° Virgo 38'
New Moons are about opening new pathways for prosperity.

Element
Earth – Practical, determined, structured, enduring, stubborn, traditional, stable, and stuck inside the box.

Statement I Heal

Body Intestines

Mind Critical/Analytical

Spirit Divinity in the Details; Loving Service

7th House Moon I Relate/I Heal

Umbrella Energy
One-on-one relationships, defines your people attraction, and how you work in relationships with the people you attract.

Karmic Awakening Fantasy/Reality

Choice Points
Action   Ancestral Strength
Non-action   Displacement

Sabian Symbol
A Fine Lace Handkerchief, Heirloom From Valorous Ancestors.

Potential
Connects us to times of victory.

Virgo Victories & Challenges

Say all of the statements in this section out loud. Then, underline the phrase that means the most to you. Use the phrase as your affirmation for manifesting throughout this moon phase.

Today, I recognize what I love most about myself. I am the source of my love, my life, and my experience. I will set aside time today to nurture myself. I allow myself to receive these gifts and know in my heart that it is natural for me to love myself. I discover, deep within myself, the knowing that the love I give myself is commensurate to the love I am willing to receive from others. I am aware that what I expect from others cannot be truly expressed or experienced if I cannot give to myself first. I can never be disappointed when I know that love is a natural resource for me today.

Today, I honor the Earth by acknowledging what she has given me. I take time out to walk in the woods or on the beach, to feel the power of the creative pulse of the creative forces flowing through my body with the energy of being alive. I spend time in my garden and plant flowers to enhance the idea of beauty today. I honor my body today and get a massage. I spend quality time sharing joyful moments with those who love to connect from the heart and realize the blessings that come from living my life with love.

Virgo Homework

Virgos manifest best through working with herbology, folk medicine, environmental industries, organic farming, recycling, horticulture, acupuncture, healing arts, nutritional counseling, yoga instruction, and editing.

The Virgo moon cycle gives birth to Divinity in its own unique way, understanding the Soul's blueprint to be a temple of beauty. This creates what is known as the "crisis of perfection" within the minds of humankind during this time. We become aware of Spirit ascending and descending at the same time and must recognize that these contradicting energies are working within us in order to give birth to Divinity.

Victory List

Acknowledge what you have overcome. Keep this list active during this moon cycle. Honoring victory allows you to accept success.

Tarot

Ask the question out loud, then draw a card. You may wish to draw it or paste a copy of it here. Then write down what you feel it might be telling you, in response to the question. Use the glossary in the appendix and record here anything about the card that captures your attention. You may wish to come back throughout the moon cycle to meditate or journal more on the card.

How is my body supporting my manifesting?

Manifesting List

This or something better than this comes to me in an easy and pleasurable way, for the good of all concerned. Thank you, Universe!

Virgo Manifesting Ideas

Now is the time to focus on manifesting a high standard of excellence, a healthy lifestyle, self-acceptance, discernment without judgment, healing abilities, a contribution to nature, and a healthy body.

New Moon in Virgo

Your Personal Moon Experience

Fill in the Cosmic Check-In page. Then look up the Moon in the chart below. Take note of the "I" statement on the outside of the wheel where the Moon is located. This is the house the Moon is in, and the statement gives you the atmospheric energy, or the "umbrella energy" of this moon phase. This becomes the first statement to use in your mantra. Then, the "I" statement that corresponds with the astrological sign the Moon is in becomes the second statement (see *Moon Notes* for this moon phase). Now, locate the same sign and degree in your personal Natal chart and make a note of the house this degree falls in. The statement that corresponds with this house becomes your third statement. Go back to the Cosmic Check-In page and circle the three statements from the charts and read what you wrote. This will give you an idea about what to expect from this moon phase on a personal level. There is a video class that shows you how to read your personal chart at www.BlueMoonAcademy.com, look for *How to Use the Moon Book*.

I Relate, I Heal, I _____.

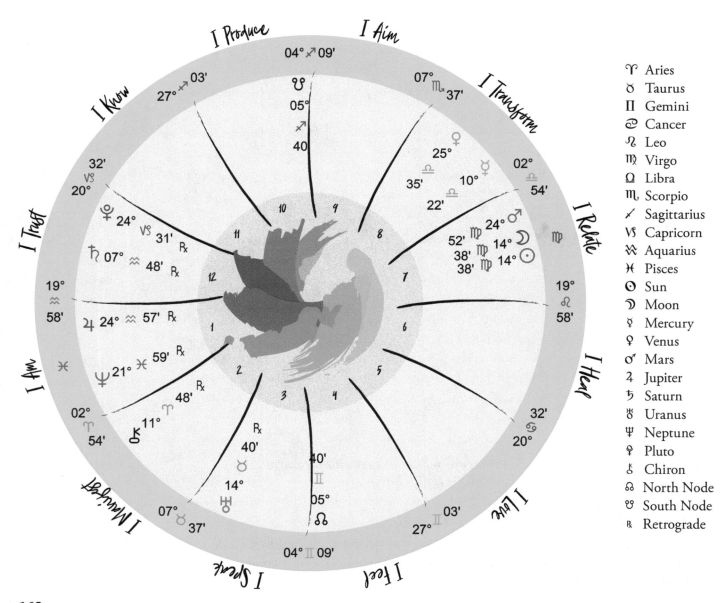

♈	Aries
♉	Taurus
♊	Gemini
♋	Cancer
♌	Leo
♍	Virgo
♎	Libra
♏	Scorpio
♐	Sagittarius
♑	Capricorn
♒	Aquarius
♓	Pisces
☉	Sun
☽	Moon
☿	Mercury
♀	Venus
♂	Mars
♃	Jupiter
♄	Saturn
♅	Uranus
♆	Neptune
♇	Pluto
⚷	Chiron
☊	North Node
☋	South Node
℞	Retrograde

Cosmic Check-In

Virgo New Moon
September 6th, 5:52 PM

Take a moment to write a brief phrase for each "I" statement. This activates all areas of your life for this creative cycle.

♍ I Heal

♎ I Relate

♏ I Transform

♐ I Aim

♑ I Produce

♒ I Know

♓ I Trust

♈ I Am

♉ I Manifest

♊ I Speak

♋ I Feel

♌ I Love

Full Moon in Pisces

September 20th, 4:55 PM

When the Sun is Opposite the Moon

Full moons are always in opposition to the Sun. This creates a feeling of tension between where you want to shine and how your feelings are flowing on a sensory level about the Sun's directive. The two forces seem like they are working against each other, yet they are on the same team displaying different techniques to obtain the same mission. The Pisces/Virgo polarity creates tension between addiction and perfection.

Pisces Goddess

Quan Yin is the personification of beneficence, serenity, healing, and unconditional love. One of the four great Bodhisattvas (enlightened ones), she was about to cross into a new dimension when she heard the cries of humanity and decided to remain on earth until all beings were enlightened. She is a protectress who brings fierce love, pouring life energy on the sorrows of the world. Pictured seated or standing on a lotus pedestal, she holds in one hand a jar that pours the elixir of life into the mouths of dragons. In the other hand, she carries a willow branch, symbol of the willingness to bend or adapt.

How can Quan Yin's unconditional love and compassion flow into your groups of friends, your families, your social circle, and your community? Her white lotus symbolizes purity, honesty, perfection, innocence and new beginnings. Recent divisiveness has polarized not only political factions, but friends and families as well. How might you set yourself free by re-aligning and adapting in the play of opposites? One tried and true way is to take Quan Yin's path to a higher level to solve the problems, through connecting with your higher self to remember your connection with the Divine. At that level we are all one, and our joys and sorrows are shared. Set aside time this moon to meditate on strengthening your awareness of your connection to The All That Is. Allow Quan Yin's compassion to flow to you, as well as to others.

Build Your Altar

Colors	Greens, blues, amethyst, aquamarine
Numerology	11 – Let truth resonate in your soul
Tarot Card	The Hanged Man – Learning to let go
Gemstones	Opal, turquoise, amethyst
Plant remedy	Passion flower – The ability to live in the here and now
Fragrance	White lotus – Connect to the Divine

Moon Notes

Full Moon 28° Pisces 14'
Full Moons are about moving beyond blocks and setting yourself free.

Element
Water – Taking the path of least resistance, going with the flow, secretive, sensual, glamorous, psychic, magnetic, escaping reality, a healer, an actor/actress, and creativity at its best.

Statement I Trust

Body Feet

Mind Fantasy

Spirit Mystical

1st House Moon I Am/I Trust

Umbrella Energy
Your outer appearance, the way you present yourself, the way you dress, the way you enter a room, and what you leave behind when you leave the room.

Karmic Awakening Fantasy/Reality

Choice Points
Action   Rewards of Wisdom
Non-action Possessive

Sabian Symbol
Light Breaking Into Many Colors As It Passes Through A Prism.

Potential
A new perception will advance your vision.

Clearing the Slate

Sixty hours before the full moon negative traits connected to the astro-sign might become activated to trigger what needs to be released during the full moon phase. You may notice a sudden urge to escape into unrealistic attitudes or addictive habits that bring a feeling of aimlessness. Make a list, look in the mirror, and for each negative trait, tell yourself *I am sorry, I forgive you, thank you for your awareness,* and *I love you.* Now is the time to start doing your Sky Power Yoga poses so your physiology can feel supported during this moon phase. The poses and the teaching are available on BlueMoonAcademy.com. Enjoy!

Pisces Victories & Challenges

Say all of the statements in this section out loud. Then, underline the phrase that means the most to you. Use the phrase as your affirmation for releasing throughout this moon phase.

The best thing I can do for myself today is to get out of the way, so life can take its own course without the interference of my control drama. I take time out to let go and let things be. I have become too involved in the details and have lost sight of the vastness of the Universe, and the infinite possibilities that are available to me at all times and in every moment. I am aware that all I need is a different way of seeing what I have perceived as a problem, and that my view is limited by my needs, rather than by accepting things as they are. I trust that, when I get out of the way and give space to the power of NOW, all is in Divine Order and everything works out for the good of all concerned. This is the day when doing nothing gets me everything. I allow myself to experience the void. I empty myself of my rigidity, small-mindedness, racing thoughts, the need to be right, and to control outcomes. I know that non-action will present me with right action. I give the Universe a chance and trust the view to be larger than mine. When I accept myself as I am, I learn what I can become. I remove myself from all of the mind chatter and allow for silence to do its work. I am aware that a quiet mind brings me peace (the absence of conflict). In turning upside down, I see how right-side-up things really are. Acceptance brings me perspective. Acceptance sets me free. Acceptance brings me wholeness. Acceptance widens my mind.

Pisces Homework

Get a foot massage to bring your energy back to the ground. Feel the power of your path on the bottom of your feet. Now that you are back to your body, it is time to make a list of the ways your boundaries get breached. After the completion of your list, read it out loud and then throw it in the ocean.

Gratitude List

Keep this list active throughout the moon cycle. This will bring you to a level of completion so that a new cycle of opportunity can occur in your life. Be prepared for miracles!

Tarot

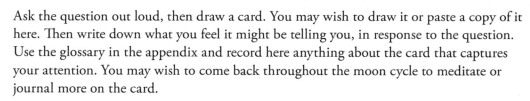

Ask the question out loud, then draw a card. You may wish to draw it or paste a copy of it here. Then write down what you feel it might be telling you, in response to the question. Use the glossary in the appendix and record here anything about the card that captures your attention. You may wish to come back throughout the moon cycle to meditate or journal more on the card.

How is my heart supporting my releasing?

Releasing List

Say this statement out loud three times before writing your list:

I am a free spiritual being and it is my desire to be free to think and to express myself fully.

From this day forward I resolve to be true — first to myself and my highest self, and then to the highest self in me which is the Source of Love That I Am.

Pisces Releasing Ideas

Now is the time to activate a game change in my life, and give up addictions, illusions and fantasy, escape dramas, martyrdom, victimhood, and mental chaos.

Full Moon in Pisces

Your Personal Moon Experience

Fill in the Cosmic Check-In page. Then look up the Moon in the chart below. Take note of the "I" statement on the outside of the wheel where the Moon is located. This is the house the Moon is in, and the statement gives you the atmospheric energy, or the "umbrella energy" of this moon phase. This becomes the first statement to use in your mantra. Then, the "I" statement that corresponds with the astrological sign the Moon is in becomes the second statement (see *Moon Notes* for this moon phase). Now, locate the same sign and degree in your personal Natal chart and make a note of the house this degree falls in. The statement that corresponds with this house becomes your third statement. Go back to the Cosmic Check-In page and circle the three statements from the charts and read what you wrote. This will give you an idea about what to expect from this moon phase on a personal level. There is a video class that shows you how to read your personal chart at www.BlueMoonAcademy.com, look for *How to Use the Moon Book*.

I Am, I Trust, I _____ .

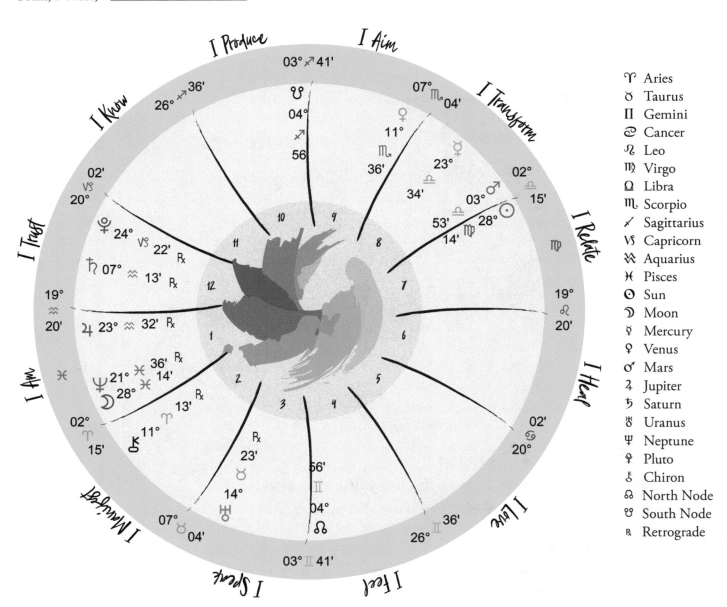

♈	Aries
♉	Taurus
♊	Gemini
♋	Cancer
♌	Leo
♍	Virgo
♎	Libra
♏	Scorpio
♐	Sagittarius
♑	Capricorn
♒	Aquarius
♓	Pisces
☉	Sun
☽	Moon
☿	Mercury
♀	Venus
♂	Mars
♃	Jupiter
♄	Saturn
♅	Uranus
♆	Neptune
♇	Pluto
⚷	Chiron
☊	North Node
☋	South Node
℞	Retrograde

Cosmic Check-In

Pisces Full Moon
September 20th, 4:55 PM

Take a moment to write a brief phrase for each "I" statement. This activates all areas of your life for this creative cycle.

♓ I Trust

♈ I Am

♉ I Manifest

♊ I Speak

♋ I Feel

♌ I Love

♍ I Heal

♎ I Relate

♏ I Transform

♐ I Aim

♑ I Produce

♒ I Know

October

Uranus is retrograde in Taurus until next year

It's working hard to bring balance to the Earth for the good of it's future.

October 1st Mercury retrograde in Libra until October 18th

Expect to be more mental than usual. Getting caught up in trying to figure anything out right now could be exhausting. Gather facts when appropriate to help you assimilate options. Time to reconcile old communications where you were misunderstood or falsely accused. See if you can live in the now rather than the land of either/or.

October 1st Jupiter retrograde in Aquarius until October 17th

Surround yourself with bright-minded people who hold the space for innovation in their consciousness. Teamwork becomes very important. Keep your intentions straight.

October 1st Saturn retrograde in Aquarius until October 10th

Use the research qualities of Saturn, the karmic technician, to determine your actions and outcomes. Watch out for spending too much time on being perfect or you may lose your space in time.

October 1st Pluto retrograde in Capricorn until October 6th

Get your money plan in order so you can start a new aspect to your business after the 6th. Be open to knowing that all your research will pay off.

October 6th – Watch out – the Sun, Moon, Mars, and Mercury retrograde are all bundled up in Libra

Expect a multilevel experience infusing you with a set of crossroads leading to a new direction and setting in a new way of reflecting all at the same time. This simultaneous experience is designed to reset your pathway to a new success. A warning comes with Mercury retrograde, "don't question it!" If you do, you lose the power of the moment and movement!

October 7th Venus moves into Sagittarius

Expect fun ... time for an adventure, dance like no one is watching. Spending could be extreme.

October 20th Mars and the Sun coupled in Libra

Expect highly charged energy here. Mars being the energizer and the Sun being the igniter will add enough rocket fuel to get you to the Moon and back. Use this wisely and a quantum leap can add to the quality of your life.

October 22nd The Sun enters Scorpio

Time to bring light to your shadow side. This is a very powerful time to look under the carpet to see where you swept the things you weren't yet ready to experience.

October 30th Mars enters Scorpio

Expect a highly-charged sexual drive.

Super Sensitivity October 10th-11th

Thinking too much could get you confused. Slow down even though the atmosphere is speeding up.

Low Vitality October 24th-25th

Be willing to move out of holding onto something that needs to be released. Remember resistance is exhausting.

SUNDAY	MONDAY	TUESDAY	WEDNESDAY	THURSDAY	FRIDAY	SATURDAY
					1☿♃♄♅♆♇℞ 4. A logical progression works.	2☿♃♄♅♆♇℞ ☽ V/C 4:42 PM 5. Take a day trip to the mountains.
3☿♃♄♅♆♇℞ ☽→♍ 1:38 AM 6. Love wins.	4☿♃♄♅♆♇℞ 7. Research brings you answers.	5☿♃♄♅♆♇℞ ☽ V/C 1:45 AM ☽→♎ 5:41 AM 8. Acknowledge your victories.	6☿♃♄♅♆℞ ● 13° ♎ 25' 4:06 AM ♇SD 24° ♑ 19' 11:29 AM ☽ V/C 10:02 PM 9. Donate your time.	7☿♃♄♅♆℞ ♀→♐ 4:21 AM ☽→♏ 7:21 AM 10. Add a new goal.	8☿♃♄♅♆℞ ☽ V/C 11:05 PM 11. Dreams find life through change.	9☿♃♄♅♆℞ ☽→♐ 8:25 AM 3. Kindness is key for joy to bloom.
10☿♃♅♆℞▲ ♄SD 6° ♒ 53' 7:17 PM ☽ V/C 9:30 PM 4. Today logic works best.	11☿♃♅♆℞▲ ☽→♑ 10:15 AM 5. Change is variation in action.	12☿♃♅♆℞ 6. Loving service opens the heart.	13☿♃♅♆℞ ☽ V/C 3:53 AM ☽→♒ 1:48 PM 7. Think outside the box today.	14☿♃♅♆℞ 8. Seeking help is powerful.	15☿♃♅♆℞ ☽ V/C 5:32 AM ☽→♓ 7:22 PM 9. Send healing energy to the Earth.	16☿♃♅♆℞ 10. Back up your devices.
17☿♅♆℞ ☽ V/C 4:23 PM ♃SD 22° ♒ 20' 10:30 PM 11. Breathe and feel your vastness.	18♅♆℞ ☽→♈ 3:04 AM ☿SD 10° ♎ 08' 8:17 AM 3. Take an optimistic attitude today.	19♅♆℞ 4. A no-nonsense, practical day.	20♅♆℞ ☽ V/C 7:56 AM ○ 27° ♈ 26' 7:57 AM ☽→♉ 12:59 PM 6. Appreciate the changing seasons.	21♅♆℞ 7. Trust that you do know.	22♅♆℞ ☽ V/C 1:35 PM ☉→♏ 9:51 PM 8. See manifestation as magical.	23♅♆℞ ☽→♊ 12:58 AM 9. Spirit expresses through creativity.
24♅♆℞▼ 10. Energy follows thought, dream big.	25♅♆℞▼ ☽ V/C 7:10 AM ☽→♋ 2:01 PM 2. Balance fact with intuition.	26♅♆℞ 3. Play creates a feel-good day.	27♅♆℞ ☽ V/C 11:01 PM 4. Is the business plan working?	28♅♆℞ ☽→♌ 2:08 AM 5. See the value in being flexible.	29♅♆℞ 6. Put on your dancing shoes.	30♅♆℞ ☽ V/C 12:04 AM ♂→♏ 7:21 AM ☽→♍ 11:10 AM 7. Solutions are easy to find.
31♅♆℞ **Halloween** 8. Make a manifestation list.						

♈ Aries	♍ Virgo	♒ Aquarius	♀ Venus	♆ Neptune	V/C Void-of-Course	2. Balance	7. Learning
♉ Taurus	♎ Libra	♓ Pisces	♂ Mars	♇ Pluto	℞ Retrograde	3. Fun	8. Money
♊ Gemini	♏ Scorpio	☉ Sun	♃ Jupiter	→ Enters	SD Stationary Direct	4. Structure	9. Spirituality
♋ Cancer	♐ Sagittarius	☽ Moon	♄ Saturn	● New Moon	▲ Super Sensitivity	5. Action	10. Visionary
♌ Leo	♑ Capricorn	☿ Mercury	♅ Uranus	○ Full Moon	▼ Low Vitality	6. Love	11. Completion

New Moon in Libra

October 6th, 4:06 AM

When the Sun is in Libra

Libra energy gives us the opportunity to bridge the gap between the higher and lower mind; abstract thinking versus concrete thinking. During Libra time, the light and dark forces are in balance and you are given a chance to experience harmony. Harmony occurs when you keep your polarities in motion and put paradox to rest, thus breaking the crystallization of polarity. Now is the time to weigh your values through the light of your Soul. Libra asks you to look at what is increasing and decreasing in your life. Start with friendship, courage, sincerity, and understanding, and keep going until your scale is in motion.

Libra Goddess

Daughter of the Sun God Re, the Egyptian Goddess Maat (pronounced Ma-yet) embodied truth, justice, righteousness, and cosmic order. The morality she personified formed the basis for the entire system of ethics and civic order for the society in Egypt. Her hieroglyph was an "M," followed by two parallel rows of five parallel lines, which meant to be just, true and direct, plus a "T," representing a feminine ending. Often pictured with an ostrich feather headdress, holding the scales of justice, she was the symbol of right action, virtue and fairness. It was believed that in the afterlife, the deceased person encountered Maat for a life review. Your heart, the Ab, would be weighed against Maat's white feather of truth. If you had been just and good, you would proceed to the afterlife.

Meditate with Maat today and ask for her help in identifying something from the past that is out of order, out of balance; something that continues to plague you. Ask her to show you the balance of your relationships with others. Is there something you do out of duty motivation or a sense of guilt? Maat calls on you to place awareness on where you are pulled or pushed to do something that is out of alignment with your true self. Allow Maat to help you break through to a more authentic way of behaving and relating, by standing up for your own highest and best good.

Build Your Altar

Colors   Pink, green

Numerology 9 – Donate your time

Tarot Card Justice – The Law of Cause and Effect

Gemstones   Jade, rose quartz

Plant Remedy Olive trees – Stamina

Fragrance   Eucalyptus – Clarity of breath

Moon Notes

New Moon   13° Libra 25'
New Moons are about opening new pathways for prosperity.

Element
Air – The breath of life that allows the mind to achieve new insights and fresh perspectives, abstract dreaming, freedom from attachments, codes of intelligence, and academic applications.

Statement I Relate

Body   Kidneys

Mind   Social

Spirit   Peace

2nd House Moon   I Manifest/I Relate

Umbrella Energy
The way you make your money and the way you spend your money.

Choice Points
Action   Cyclical Opportunities
Non-action   Mental Looping

Sabian Symbol
Circular Paths.

Potential
Creative pathways opening.

Libra Victories & Challenges

Say all of the statements in this section out loud. Then, underline the phrase that means the most to you. Use the phrase as your affirmation for manifesting throughout this moon phase.

I feel the call of the higher worlds awakening me to a new vibration. This call is to move beyond judgment and move to a place of acceptance, understanding, unconditional confidence, and love. I am at a place in my life where I can embrace the world of acceptance and wholeness, because I have birthed myself anew, beyond the imprisonment and crystallization of polarity and righteousness. My black and white worlds of right and wrong have integrated and blended into gray, the color of wisdom, where true knowledge exists. Knowledge simply is, and the need for proof does not exist where wisdom lives.

The only requirement is experience. I know that everything that comes before me is a direct reflection of my own experience and, in embracing this concept, I can now receive the gift of infinite awareness. I am in a place of awareness that came before and goes beyond where good and evil exist. I have within me, the presence of unconditional confidence to go where true love lives. I no longer need to prove myself. I am now simply being myself. I release the need to be right and accept the right to BE. I no longer need to be forgiven, because I am neither wrong nor right. I no longer need to define myself. Acceptance has no reason for defense. I no longer need to be guilty; duty motivation is no longer a reality. I know that where there is judgment, there is separation. I know understanding unifies. I accept the call of the higher worlds and express myself freely and fully without fear of judgment. I accept myself as I am, so I can learn what I can become.

Libra Homework

Libras manifest best through the legal industry, beauty industry, diplomatic service, match-making, urban development, mediation, feng shui, spa ownership, clutter-busting and space clearing, romance writing, wedding consulting, fashion design, and as librarians.

It is time to weigh and measure the values of relationship, friendship, courage, sensitivity, sincerity, and understanding. Look at what is increasing and what is decreasing in these areas.

177

Victory List

Acknowledge what you have overcome. Keep this list active during this moon cycle. Honoring victory allows you to accept success.

Tarot

Ask the question out loud, then draw a card. You may wish to draw it or paste a copy of it here. Then write down what you feel it might be telling you, in response to the question. Use the glossary in the appendix and record here anything about the card that captures your attention. You may wish to come back throughout the moon cycle to meditate or journal more on the card.

How is my mind supporting my manifesting?

Manifesting List

This or something better than this comes to me in an easy and pleasurable way, for the good of all concerned. Thank you, Universe!

Libra Manifesting Ideas

Now is the time to focus on manifesting relationships, wholeness, being loving, lovable, and loved, living life as an art form, balance and equality, integrity, accuracy, diplomacy, and peace.

New Moon in Libra

Your Personal Moon Experience

Fill in the Cosmic Check-In page. Then look up the Moon in the chart below. Take note of the "I" statement on the outside of the wheel where the Moon is located. This is the house the Moon is in, and the statement gives you the atmospheric energy, or the "umbrella energy" of this moon phase. This becomes the first statement to use in your mantra. Then, the "I" statement that corresponds with the astrological sign the Moon is in becomes the second statement (see *Moon Notes* for this moon phase). Now, locate the same sign and degree in your personal Natal chart and make a note of the house this degree falls in. The statement that corresponds with this house becomes your third statement. Go back to the Cosmic Check-In page and circle the three statements from the charts and read what you wrote. This will give you an idea about what to expect from this moon phase on a personal level. There is a video class that shows you how to read your personal chart at www.BlueMoonAcademy.com, look for *How to Use the Moon Book*.

I Manifest, I Relate, I _____ .

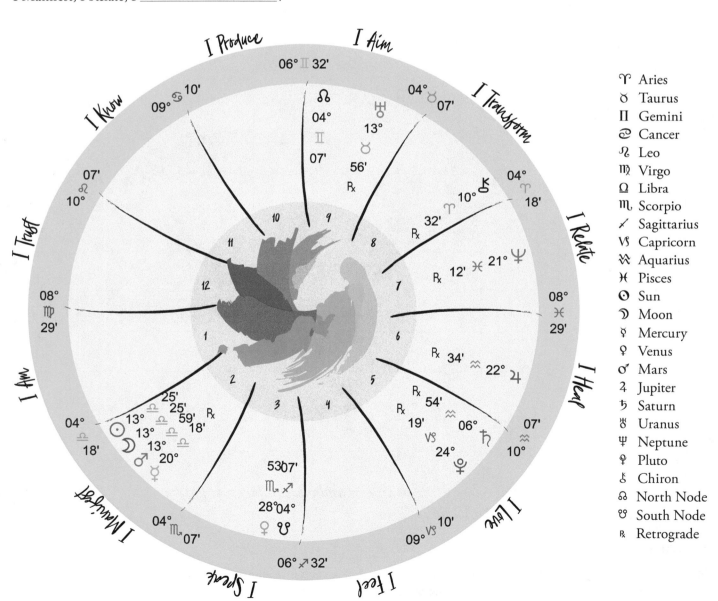

♈	Aries
♉	Taurus
♊	Gemini
♋	Cancer
♌	Leo
♍	Virgo
♎	Libra
♏	Scorpio
♐	Sagittarius
♑	Capricorn
♒	Aquarius
♓	Pisces
☉	Sun
☽	Moon
☿	Mercury
♀	Venus
♂	Mars
♃	Jupiter
♄	Saturn
♅	Uranus
♆	Neptune
♀	Pluto
⚷	Chiron
☊	North Node
☋	South Node
℞	Retrograde

Cosmic Check-In

Libra New Moon
October 6th, 4:06 AM

Take a moment to write a brief phrase for each "I" statement. This activates all areas of your life for this creative cycle.

♎ I Relate

♏ I Transform

♐ I Aim

♑ I Produce

♒ I Know

♓ I Trust

♈ I Am

♉ I Manifest

♊ I Speak

♋ I Feel

♌ I Love

♍ I Heal

Full Moon in Aries

October 20th, 7:57 AM

When the Sun is Opposite the Moon

Full moons are always in opposition to the Sun. This creates a feeling of tension between where you want to shine and how your feelings are flowing on a sensory level about the Sun's directive. The two forces seem like they are working against each other, yet they are on the same team displaying different techniques to obtain the same mission. The Aries/Libra polarity creates tension between "I Am" and "We Are".

Aries Goddess

Artemis (Roman Diana), "The Shining One," Goddess of the Moon and the Hunt, silently takes her perfect aim with her silver bow and golden arrow to help you focus your energies. Well known as Huntress as well as protector of the land and all its creatures, Artemis was also renown as a powerful sorceress. She appeared in darkened forest groves at the new moon to bless her creatures and to call down the moon to begin its journey to fullness. That full moon is now here with its light in the darkness. Time to power up your crystals in the moonlight overnight. Aries sets our souls aflame with the archetype of the physically fit, fiercely independent, passionate and confident leader. The physical world was Artemis's domain where she patrolled the earth, fully embodied and empowered, beholden to none. It was said she had a radiant confidence that came from her glowing inner light within. What does Artemis trigger within your body? Allow her to reinvigorate and re-energize your inner light, just as the moonlight charges your crystals with a power ineffable. Dare to go out and dance in the moonlight and feel your connection to Mother Earth through your bare feet. Take aim at a goal you thought impossible! Take the lead in a project dear to your heart. As the quote goes, "Shoot for the Moon. Even if you miss, you'll land among the Stars!"

Build Your Altar

Colors	Red, black, coral
Numerology	6 – Appreciate the changing seasons
Tarot Card	Tower – Release from a stuck place, major breakthrough
Gemstones	Diamond, red jasper, coral, obsidian
Plant remedy	Oak, pomegranate – Planting and rooting new life
Fragrance	Ginger – The ability to ingest and digest life

Moon Notes

Full Moon   27° Aries 26'
Full Moons are about moving beyond blocks and setting yourself free.

Element
Fire – Igniting, dissolving, accelerating, cleansing, advancing awareness, impatience, leadership, passion, and vitality.

Statement   I Am

Body   Head

Mind   Ego-centric

Spirit   Leadership

6th House Moon   I Heal/I Am

Umbrella Energy
The way you manage your body and its appearance.

Choice Points
Action   Spiritual Independence
Non-action   Transient Reward

Sabian Symbol
A Large Audience Confronts The Performer Who Disappointed Its Expectations.

Potential
Facing reality about standard of excellence.

Clearing the Slate

Sixty hours before the full moon negative traits connected to the astro-sign might become activated to trigger what needs to be released during the full moon phase. You may notice a sudden need to be first or impatience that could lead to anger or arrogance. Make a list, look in the mirror, and for each negative trait, tell yourself *I am sorry, I forgive you, thank you for your awareness,* and *I love you.* Now is the time to start doing your Sky Power Yoga poses so your physiology can feel supported during this moon phase. The poses and the teaching are available on BlueMoonAcademy.com. Enjoy!

Aries Victories & Challenges

Say all of the statements in this section out loud. Then, underline the phrase that means the most to you. Use the phrase as your affirmation for releasing throughout this moon phase.

Today, I let go. I trust that whatever breaks down or breaks through is a blessing in disguise for me. I make a commitment to allow myself to be spontaneous and live in the moment. I know the unexpected is a blessing for me and a way for me to make a breakthrough out of my limitations. I am aware that I am resistant to change. I know I must make changes and am too stubborn to take the appropriate action myself to change. I have built many walls of false protection around me, guarding me and blocking me from the reality that change is a constant. I have freeze-framed my life and desire support to update myself. I have allowed my fear of change to become my false motto and my life is at a standstill. I am unwilling to use any more energy to perpetuate my resistance. I know that continuing to cling to the past is a waste of my energy. I can no longer put things off that delay my process. I feel the breaking down of form. I trust that all changes are in my favor. All changes lead me to golden opportunities. I release false pride. I release false foundations. I release false authorities. In so doing, I allow for everything to crumble around me so I can see that my true strength is within and I will build my life from the inside out.

I am ready for new experiences. I am ready for the unexpected. I am willing to have an event occur so I can become activated towards my breakthrough. I am ready for the power of now. I know being spontaneous will bring me to true joy. I know if I ride this carrier wave it will take me to a place far beyond my scope of limited thinking. I know the will of God works in my favor and knows more than I do in any given moment.

Aries Homework

Now you are ready to take a personal inventory on behaviors such as impatience, talking over people, brat attacks, and starting every sentence with "I."

This is a time when the light becomes a prisoner of polarized forces. This diminishing light begins its yearly sojourn beneath the surface, asking us to balance light and dark by mastering the concept of equilibrium. Equilibrium is the Law of Harmony, where we attempt to reach a state of achievement by combining paradoxical fields that break the crystallization of polarity. Spend time looking for increasing and decreasing fields of light around you.

Gratitude List

Keep this list active throughout the moon cycle. This will bring you to a level of completion so that a new cycle of opportunity can occur in your life. Be prepared for miracles!

Tarot

Ask the question out loud, then draw a card. You may wish to draw it or paste a copy of it here. Then write down what you feel it might be telling you, in response to the question. Use the glossary in the appendix and record here anything about the card that captures your attention. You may wish to come back throughout the moon cycle to meditate or journal more on the card.

How is my spirit supporting my releasing?

Releasing List

Say this statement out loud three times before writing your list:

*I am a free spiritual being and it is my desire to be free to think
and to express myself fully.*

*From this day forward I resolve to be true — first to myself and my highest self,
and then to the highest self in me which is the Source of Love That I Am.*

Aries Releasing Ideas

Now is the time to activate a game change in my life, and give up anger as a default,
competition and comparison, irritation and struggle, the need to be first, overdoing it and
not resting, impatience, impulsiveness, and hostility.

Full Moon in Aries

Your Personal Moon Experience

Fill in the Cosmic Check-In page. Then look up the Moon in the chart below. Take note of the "I" statement on the outside of the wheel where the Moon is located. This is the house the Moon is in, and the statement gives you the atmospheric energy, or the "umbrella energy" of this moon phase. This becomes the first statement to use in your mantra. Then, the "I" statement that corresponds with the astrological sign the Moon is in becomes the second statement (see *Moon Notes* for this moon phase). Now, locate the same sign and degree in your personal Natal chart and make a note of the house this degree falls in. The statement that corresponds with this house becomes your third statement. Go back to the Cosmic Check-In page and circle the three statements from the charts and read what you wrote. This will give you an idea about what to expect from this moon phase on a personal level. There is a video class that shows you how to read your personal chart at www.BlueMoonAcademy.com, look for *How to Use the Moon Book*.

I Heal, I Am, I _____ .

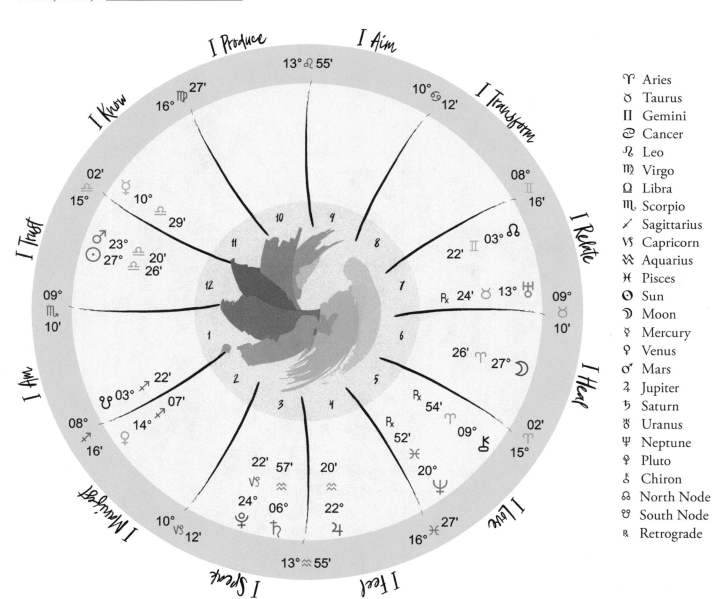

♈	Aries
♉	Taurus
♊	Gemini
♋	Cancer
♌	Leo
♍	Virgo
♎	Libra
♏	Scorpio
♐	Sagittarius
♑	Capricorn
♒	Aquarius
♓	Pisces
☉	Sun
☽	Moon
☿	Mercury
♀	Venus
♂	Mars
♃	Jupiter
♄	Saturn
♅	Uranus
♆	Neptune
♇	Pluto
⚷	Chiron
☊	North Node
☋	South Node
℞	Retrograde

Cosmic Check-In

Aries Full Moon
October 20th, 7:57 AM

Take a moment to write a brief phrase for each "I" statement. This activates all areas of your life for this creative cycle.

♈ I Am

♉ I Manifest

♊ I Speak

♋ I Feel

♌ I Love

♍ I Heal

♎ I Relate

♏ I Transform

♐ I Aim

♑ I Produce

♒ I Know

♓ I Trust

November

Uranus is retrograde in Taurus until next year

This connection is very important because Uranus' influence is smoothing out and streamlining the Earth for the future. The concept of global warming has to be dealt with as a future focus that only Uranus can provide. Uranus is all about preparing Earth for the transformation of the decade.

Neptune is retrograde in Pisces until December 1st

At this time, we are doing our best to set ourselves free from the imprisonment of our past disappointments and broken dreams. Now is the time to face reality and get that the dream had no grounding or any connection to reality. So, we must take responsibility for the lack of connection and move on. Remember, it is no longer fashionable to be a martyr or a victim.

November 4th Sun/Moon conjunct in Scorpio

Time to put new action or direction into your life. Your memories are ready to be released. The action of doing this will lead you to a new adventure far beyond your wildest dreams.

November 4th Mercury and Mars coupled in Scorpio and Libra

These two planets are scratching the surface and annoying each other on a subject that is long overdue. Use this to get rid of a long-term question or belief about relationship. It is no longer fashionable to hold on to this. Time to learn the new paradigm for relating.

November 5th Venus enters Capricorn

Yucky for Venus. She is forced at this time to be practical.

November 5th Mercury enters Scorpio

If you have any secrets to share with someone, now is the time. Trust that whatever you say during this transit, it will be kept a secret throughout eternity.

November 19th The Moon conjunct the North Node

Time to focus on your future direction. What you have been longing for will get total support.

November 19th The Sun and Mercury Conjunct in Scorpio

The light shines on your shadow side. Set yourself free from what you have wanted to say for a really long time.

November 21st The Sun enters Sagittarius

Party time! As the light hits the ground you will start running towards the nearest form of fun and adventure.

November 24th Mercury enters Sagittarius

Watch out for 'foot-in-mouth disease.' You may find out that too much talking can get you in trouble. Before speaking ask yourself, "Is it kind? Is it truthful? Is it necessary?"

Super Sensitivity November 3rd-8th

Venus is over the sensitivity fixed star. Watch what you say as you could hurt someone's ego. Also, worry could take over and if it does, ask yourself where you have forgotten to take action.

Low Vitality November 21st-22nd

See what you can do to take it easy over the holidays for a change. Perhaps you will have more fun if you are not exhausted.

SUNDAY	MONDAY	TUESDAY	WEDNESDAY	THURSDAY	FRIDAY	SATURDAY
	1 ♅♉♆℞ ☽ V/C 10:00 AM ☽→♎ 4:11 PM 9. Spirit speaks through children.	2 ♅♉♆℞ 10. Vision requires active intention.	3 ♅♉♆℞▲ ☽ V/C 3:32 PM ☽→♏ 5:53 PM 11. As above, so below.	4 ♅♉♆℞▲ ● 12° ♏ 40' 2:15 PM 3. Relish those playful moments.	5 ♅♉♆℞▲ ♀→♑ 3:43 AM ☽ V/C 9:09 AM ☿→♏ 3:34 PM ☽→♐ 5:53 PM 4. To be sensible has its rewards.	6 ♅♉♆℞▲ 5. Diversity encourages new choices.
7 ♅♉♆℞▲ PST begins 2:00 AM ☽ V/C 5:43 AM ☽→♑ 5:03 PM 6. Share love, be love.	8 ♅♉♆℞▲ 7. Trust your insights.	9 ♅♉♆℞ ☽ V/C 9:51 AM ☽→♒ 7:02 PM 8. Prosperity rules the day!	10 ♅♉♆℞ 9. You are a spiritual being.	11 ♅♉♆℞ **Veteran's Day** ☽ V/C 11:52 AM ☽→♓ 11:54 PM 10. Move forward with courage.	12 ♅♉♆℞ 2. Decisions go in your favor.	13 ♅♉♆℞ ☽ V/C 9:39 PM 3. The tool of the day is creativity.
14 ♅♉♆℞ ☽→♈ 7:48 AM 4. The plan requires a logical touch.	15 ♅♉♆℞ 5. Change is your friend today.	16 ♅♉♆℞ ☽ V/C 7:50 AM ☽→♉ 6:18 PM 6. Energy improves with body care.	17 ♅♉♆℞ 7. Search for new recipes.	18 ♅♉♆℞ 8. Allow cycles to create new success.	19 ♅♉♆℞ ☽ V/C 12:57 AM ○ 27° ♉ 14' 12:58 AM **Lunar Eclipse** 27° ♉ 17' 1:03 AM ☽→♊ 6:33 AM 9. Service brings joy.	20 ♅♉♆℞ 10. A large vision supports big goals.
21 ♅♉♆℞▼ ☉→♐ 6:33 PM ☽ V/C 7:51 AM ☽→♋ 7:33 PM 2. Harmony requires adaptability.	22 ♅♉♆℞▼ 3. The energy today enhances optimism.	23 ♅♉♆℞ ☽ V/C 9:45 PM 4. Slow down and pay attention.	24 ♅♉♆℞ ☿→♐ 7:36 AM ☽→♌ 7:59 AM 5. Plan a new adventure.	25 ♅♉♆℞ **Thanksgiving** 6. Be thankful for all your blessings.	26 ♅♉♆℞ ☽ V/C 8:23 AM ☽→♍ 6:11 PM 7. Teach what you have learned.	27 ♅♉♆℞ 8. Your success begins with variety.
28 ♅♉♆℞ **Chanukah Begins at Sunset** ☽ V/C 4:02 PM 9. Spirituality knows no bounds.	29 ♅♉♆℞ ☽→♎ 12:55 AM 10. A day for innovation and progress.	30 ♅♉♆℞ ☽ V/C 8:19 PM 2. Intuition speaks loudly today.				

♈ Aries	♍ Virgo	♒ Aquarius	♀ Venus	♆ Neptune	V/C Void-of-Course	2. Balance	7. Learning
♉ Taurus	♎ Libra	♓ Pisces	♂ Mars	♇ Pluto	℞ Retrograde	3. Fun	8. Money
♊ Gemini	♏ Scorpio	☉ Sun	♃ Jupiter	→ Enters	SD Stationary Direct	4. Structure	9. Spirituality
♋ Cancer	♐ Sagittarius	☽ Moon	♄ Saturn	● New Moon	▲ Super Sensitivity	5. Action	10. Visionary
♌ Leo	♑ Capricorn	☿ Mercury	♅ Uranus	○ Full Moon	▼ Low Vitality	6. Love	11. Completion

New Moon in Scorpio

November 4th, 2:15 PM

When the Sun is in Scorpio

Scorpio is the symbol of darkness which heralds the decline of the Sun in Autumn. As we watch all of nature going through a slow death, we begin to recognize the qualities of Scorpio's subtlety and depth, and the hidden forces that threaten those who live only on the surface. Scorpio rules all of the things that you try to keep hidden: ambition, pride, and fear. When you face these self-imposed limits on yourself, you take on the true power of transformation.

Scorpio Goddess

Goddess of Underworld and death, war and fate, the Irish "Phantom Queen" flies in this dark moon on silent crow wings. A fierce guardian of her territory and its people, the Morrigan is defender and protector. She also is a diviner and seer, famous for predicting fortunes won and lost on the battlefield. She is said to be a shape-shifter and trickster, appearing as a crow as an omen of death. Ancient traditions tell of "The Morrigan" as a trio of Celtic goddesses, named Eriu, Banba and Fodla; or sisters, Badb, Macha and Nemain. "Eriu's land" became "Ireland"; Badb was the name of the crow who came to signal death before a battle, and Nemain meant panic or frenzy. Their origins go back to Copper Age Megalithic Cults of the Mother Goddess. Formidable indeed, The Morrigan asks you to be vigilant, wary and watch, so you will know when to take action. The Morrigan will help you shape-shift to align with the times and circumstances. She comes when righteous anger arises, and our children and the earth need protecting. Her songs reverberate in our chests and nurture through our breasts. Weary of injustice, she rises! Tired of pain and suffering, she rises! Grieving deaths and attending the dying, she rises! The Morrigan asks you to transmute loss and pain, to mourn, to defend and protect the downtrodden. She asks you to stand up for your truth. She teaches that magic is our ability to control, change and master ourselves before we take up the battle to change the world, one step at a time.

Build Your Altar

Colors	Deep red, black, deep purple
Numerology	3 – Relish those playful moments
Tarot Card	Death – Transform, transmute, and transcend
Gemstones	Topaz, smoky quartz, obsidian, jet, onyx
Plant Remedy	Manzanita – Being open to transforming cycles
Fragrance	Sandalwood – Awakens your sensuality

Moon Notes

New Moon   12° Scorpio 40'
New Moons are about opening new pathways for prosperity.

Element
Water – Taking the path of least resistance, going with the flow, secretive, sensual, glamorous, psychic, magnetic, escaping reality, a healer, an actor/actress, and creativity at its best.

Statement   I Transform

Body   Reproductive Organs

Mind   Sexual focus

Spirit   Transformation

9th House Moon   I Aim/I Transform

Umbrella Energy
The way you approach spirituality, philosophy, journeys, higher knowledge, and aspiration.

Choice Points
Action   Inventiveness
Non-action   Pointless Goals

Sabian Symbol
An Inventor Performs A Laboratory Experiment.

Potential
Advancement through trial and error.

Scorpio Victories & Challenges

Say all of the statements in this section out loud. Then, underline the phrase that means the most to you. Use the phrase as your affirmation for manifesting throughout this moon phase.

"When the student needs to learn, the teacher appears." Today, I recognize that the Law of Reflection is in operation. I have become aware of this through my over-indulgence of judgment and criticism of other people. I am aware that when my judgment is running rampant, I am in need of a teacher who can interpret this judgment as reflection, so I can see my judgments as my teachers and use them to re-interpret myself. I seek counsel with someone who has the ability to listen to me, hear me, and give me the space I need to see myself. I have become confused by spending too much time looking outside of myself for the answers. Perhaps my authority systems, like my religion or my family traditions, no longer serve me and I need to use this confusion to become aware of a new, more self-reliant way to live my life.

The Law of Reflection

Whatever I judge is what I am, what I fear, or what I lack. I make a list of my judgments:

I rewrite each judgment in the form of a question:
Am I _____? Do I fear _____? Do I lack _____?

Example 1: I judge Mary's wealth. Do I fear wealth? Do I lack wealth? Am I wealthy in my own way and forgetting to acknowledge my own ability to manifest?

Example 2: I judge John's "be perfect" attitude. Do I fear perfection? Do I lack perfection? Have I forgotten to recognize my own perfection?

In moving through this process, I reconnect to myself and find my own authority today. I send blessings to others whose reflection has so beautifully shown me myself today. I now know and cherish my judgments as my greatest teachers and set myself free today.

Scorpio Homework

Scorpios manifest best by being a private investigator, detective, probate attorney, mystery writer, mythologist, Tarot reader, symbolist, hospice worker, transition counselor, mortician, sex surrogate, or in forensic medicine.

The Scorpio moon cycle asks you to transform. In order to do this you must transmute sex drive into creativity, physical comfort into serving the greater good, money into higher value, fear into light, animosity into understanding, ambition into service to beauty, pride into humility, separation into unity, control into harmony, and power into empowerment.

Victory List

Acknowledge what you have overcome. Keep this list active during this moon cycle. Honoring victory allows you to accept success.

Tarot

Ask the question out loud, then draw a card. You may wish to draw it or paste a copy of it here. Then write down what you feel it might be telling you, in response to the question. Use the glossary in the appendix and record here anything about the card that captures your attention. You may wish to come back throughout the moon cycle to meditate or journal more on the card.

How is my heart supporting my manifesting?

Manifesting List

This or something better than this comes to me in an easy and pleasurable way, for the good of all concerned. Thank you, Universe!

Scorpio Manifesting Ideas

Now is the time to focus on manifesting transformation on all levels, bringing light to the dark, knowing and living cycles, knowing trust as an option, accepting change, accepting my sexuality, knowing sex is natural, knowing sex as good, and knowing sex as creative.

197

New Moon in Scorpio

Your Personal Moon Experience

Fill in the Cosmic Check-In page. Then look up the Moon in the chart below. Take note of the "I" statement on the outside of the wheel where the Moon is located. This is the house the Moon is in, and the statement gives you the atmospheric energy, or the "umbrella energy" of this moon phase. This becomes the first statement to use in your mantra. Then, the "I" statement that corresponds with the astrological sign the Moon is in becomes the second statement (see *Moon Notes* for this moon phase). Now, locate the same sign and degree in your personal Natal chart and make a note of the house this degree falls in. The statement that corresponds with this house becomes your third statement. Go back to the Cosmic Check-In page and circle the three statements from the charts and read what you wrote. This will give you an idea about what to expect from this moon phase on a personal level. There is a video class that shows you how to read your personal chart at www.BlueMoonAcademy.com, look for *How to Use the Moon Book*.

I Aim, I Transform, I _____ .

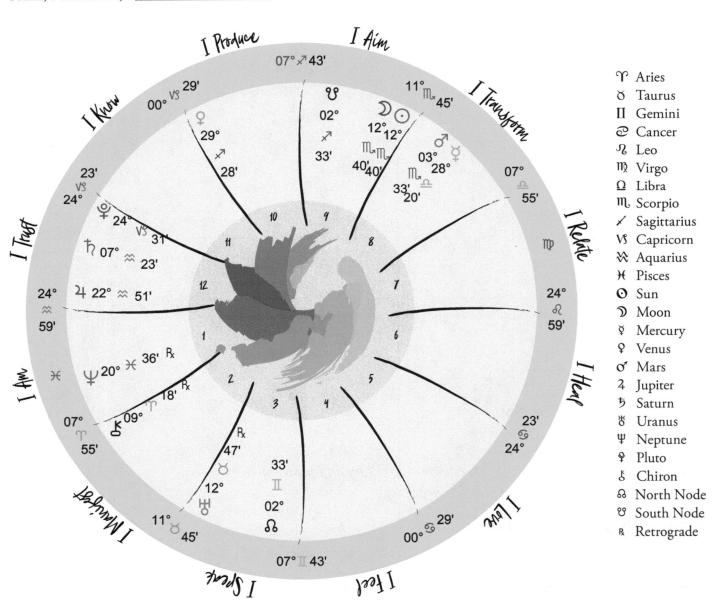

♈	Aries
♉	Taurus
♊	Gemini
♋	Cancer
♌	Leo
♍	Virgo
♎	Libra
♏	Scorpio
♐	Sagittarius
♑	Capricorn
♒	Aquarius
♓	Pisces
☉	Sun
☽	Moon
☿	Mercury
♀	Venus
♂	Mars
♃	Jupiter
♄	Saturn
♅	Uranus
♆	Neptune
♀	Pluto
⚷	Chiron
☊	North Node
☋	South Node
℞	Retrograde

Cosmic Check-In

Scorpio New Moon
November 4th, 2:15 PM

Take a moment to write a brief phrase for each "I" statement. This activates all areas of your life for this creative cycle.

♏ I Transform

♐ I Aim

♑ I Produce

♒ I Know

♓ I Trust

♈ I Am

♉ I Manifest

♊ I Speak

♋ I Feel

♌ I Love

♍ I Heal

♎ I Relate

Full Moon in Taurus

November 19th, 12:58 AM

When the Sun is Opposite the Moon

Full moons are always in opposition to the Sun. This creates a feeling of tension between where you want to shine and how your feelings are flowing on a sensory level about the Sun's directive. The two forces seem like they are working against each other, yet they are on the same team displaying different techniques to obtain the same mission. The Taurus/Scorpio polarity creates tension between "my" money and "our" money.

Taurus Goddess

Freyja, Norse goddess of love, beauty, fertility, sex, and war, was another trickster. Her name in Old Norse means, "The Lady." Stories tell of her famous golden necklace or gleaming torc named "Brisingamen," and a chariot pulled by two cats, accompanied by a wild boar, Hildisvini. She had a cloak of falcon feathers that enabled her to fly. Half of those lost in battle go to her hall, Folkvangr, while the other half go to Odin in Valhalla. Feisty, lusty stories of Freyja abound, where she even bests Loki in an insult throwing contest and pulls stunts with Thor. When she heard of the exquisite golden necklace, she just had to have it. She offered money and other gifts, but the dwarves who made it would only give it to her if she agreed to have sex with them. She bawdily agreed and carried through.

Checking off all the boxes, Frejya as a Taurus goddess in the story of her bling is right on target. The neck represents the part of the body associated with Taurus, the mind is fixated on collecting, the spirit on accumulation. Its all about how you manage your physical form and your appearance. It's easy to imagine her arriving in her chariot dressed only in her falcon feather cloak and gleaming golden torc. That kind of brass and bravado, unapologetic sexuality, unafraid to play with the big boys is admirable to a point. A good tradition to start this holiday season is to make the first present you buy for yourself. Treat yourself to something that will make you feel pretty, sexy and just a little flirtatious. Something to honor your inner light in the season of bling.

Build Your Altar

Colors	Scarlet, earth tones
Numerology	9 – Service brings joy
Tarot Card	Hierophant – Spiritual authority
Gemstones	Red coral, red agate, garnet
Plant remedy	Angelica – Connecting Heaven and Earth
Fragrance	Rose – Opening the heart

Moon Notes

Full Moon   27° Taurus 14'
Full Moons are about moving beyond blocks and setting yourself free.

Lunar Eclipse   1:03 AM

Element
Earth – Practical, determined, structured, enduring, stubborn, traditional, stable, and stuck inside the box.

Statement   I Manifest

Body   Neck

Mind   Collecting

Spirit   Accumulation

9th House Moon   I Aim/I Manifest

Umbrella Energy
The way you approach spirituality, philosophy, journeys, higher knowledge, and aspiration.

Choice Points
Action   New Passion
Non-action   Settling For Less

Sabian Symbol
A Woman, Past Her "Change Of Life", Experiences A New Love.

Potential
Love has no limits.

Clearing the Slate

Sixty hours before the full moon negative traits connected to the astro-sign might become activated to trigger what needs to be released during the full moon phase. You may notice a sudden unwillingness to share or find yourself being stubborn, wasteful, or resisting change. Make a list, look in the mirror, and for each negative trait, tell yourself *I am sorry, I forgive you, thank you for your awareness, and I love you.* Now is the time to start doing your Sky Power Yoga poses so your physiology can feel supported during this moon phase. The poses and the teaching are available on BlueMoonAcademy.com. Enjoy!

Taurus Victories & Challenges

Say all of the statements in this section out loud. Then, underline the phrase that means the most to you. Use the phrase as your affirmation for releasing throughout this moon phase.

Everything is possible for me today. My possibilities are endless. I have the power within me to make all of my dreams come true. I have the tools to make my talent a reality. I have the power to identify with my talent. Today, I focus my attention and intention on manifesting with my talent and, in so doing, I transform my ideas into reality. I recognize the part of me that is connected to the cosmic source of ideas and I express that source within me to manifest my creative power. I see my possibilities and act on them today. I am the creative power. I am all-knowing. I am an individual. There is no one else like me. I can manifest anything I desire. I intend it, I allow it, so be it.

Rules for Manifesting

Know what you want. Write it down. Say it out loud. Recognize that because you thought it, it can be so. Release your limiting beliefs. Override your limiting beliefs with power statements. Act as if you have already manifested your idea. Lastly, value yourself!

Taurus Homework

Taureans manifest best when buying, selling, and owning real estate, gardening and landscaping, selling and collecting art, manufacturing and selling fine furniture, singing or acting, and as a restaurateur, antique dealer, or interior designer.

The Taurus moon asks us to infuse light into form and, in so doing, the bridge between humanity and divinity is actualized and we can assume our stewardship in the physical world. When we release Spirit into matter, we become open to the idea that accumulation and actualization set us free to experience the abundance available to us here on Earth. Go shopping!

Gratitude List

Keep this list active throughout the moon cycle. This will bring you to a level of completion so that a new cycle of opportunity can occur in your life. Be prepared for miracles!

Tarot

Ask the question out loud, then draw a card. You may wish to draw it or paste a copy of it here. Then write down what you feel it might be telling you, in response to the question. Use the glossary in the appendix and record here anything about the card that captures your attention. You may wish to come back throughout the moon cycle to meditate or journal more on the card.

How is my body supporting my releasing?

Releasing List

Say this statement out loud three times before writing your list:

I am a free spiritual being and it is my desire to be free to think and to express myself fully.

From this day forward I resolve to be true — first to myself and my highest self, and then to the highest self in me which is the Source of Love That I Am.

Taurus Releasing Ideas

Now is the time to activate a game change in my life, and give up envy, financial insecurity, being stubborn, hoarding, addictive spending, not feeling valuable, and fear of change.

Full Moon in Taurus

Your Personal Moon Experience

Fill in the Cosmic Check-In page. Then look up the Moon in the chart below. Take note of the "I" statement on the outside of the wheel where the Moon is located. This is the house the Moon is in, and the statement gives you the atmospheric energy, or the "umbrella energy" of this moon phase. This becomes the first statement to use in your mantra. Then, the "I" statement that corresponds with the astrological sign the Moon is in becomes the second statement (see *Moon Notes* for this moon phase). Now, locate the same sign and degree in your personal Natal chart and make a note of the house this degree falls in. The statement that corresponds with this house becomes your third statement. Go back to the Cosmic Check-In page and circle the three statements from the charts and read what you wrote. This will give you an idea about what to expect from this moon phase on a personal level. There is a video class that shows you how to read your personal chart at www.BlueMoonAcademy.com, look for *How to Use the Moon Book*.

I Aim, I Manifest, I _____ .

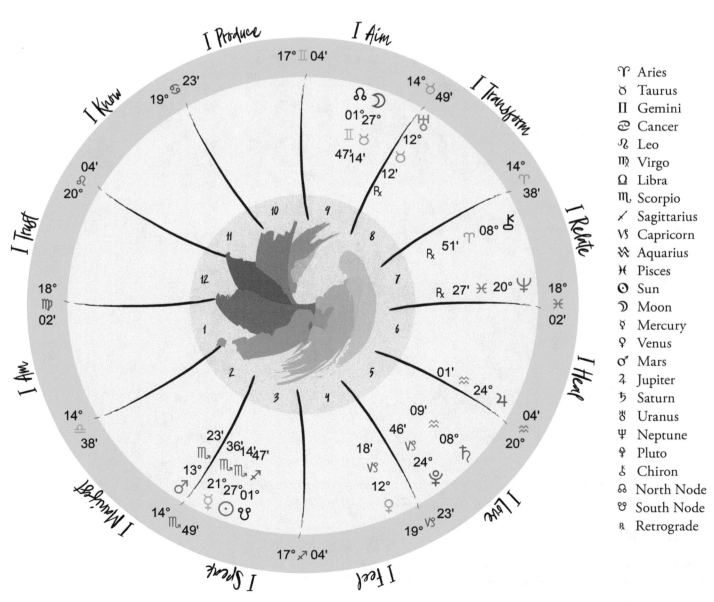

♈	Aries
♉	Taurus
♊	Gemini
♋	Cancer
♌	Leo
♍	Virgo
♎	Libra
♏	Scorpio
♐	Sagittarius
♑	Capricorn
♒	Aquarius
♓	Pisces
☉	Sun
☽	Moon
☿	Mercury
♀	Venus
♂	Mars
♃	Jupiter
♄	Saturn
♅	Uranus
♆	Neptune
♇	Pluto
⚷	Chiron
☊	North Node
☋	South Node
℞	Retrograde

Cosmic Check-In

Taurus Full Moon
November 19th, 12:58 AM

Take a moment to write a brief phrase for each "I" statement. This activates all areas of your life for this creative cycle.

♉ I Manifest

♊ I Speak

♋ I Feel

♌ I Love

♍ I Heal

♎ I Relate

♏ I Transform

♐ I Aim

♑ I Produce

♒ I Know

♓ I Trust

♈ I Am

December

December 1st Neptune goes direct in Pisces

You may feel an uplift from this emotional overload. Be willing to find the joy in your discoveries from the last few months.

December 1st Uranus retrograde continues throughout the entire month

The Earth still may wobble a bit while it is pulling the wrinkles out of the landscapes. Let it be and hold the space for the transformational decade to come into more fullness.

December 3rd Venus and Pluto are coupled in Capricorn throughout the entire month

The need for deeper versions of intimacy will be in operation. Dancing can help smooth this out if roughness occurs. A shopping spree will also help for both of you. The more expensive, the better the outcome.

December 3rd The Sun, Moon, and Mercury tripled in Sagittarius

This is a time when blending these levels of your personal self could really get you moving in the right direction. Your inner and outer realities are integrating, adding to a reality of personal development. The more you talk about it, the better it manifests.

December 3rd Solar Eclipse in Sagittarius

Take a good look at what you were representing during 2002 and the uncomfortable parts will be released into perpetuity.

December 13th Mars enters Sagittarius

At long last Mars gets to land in a place where he can go full blast. Nothing can stop him now! Travel comes to the top of the wish list. Adventure is in the air and ready to play. Go now! Act on this before the 19th and all will be well.

December 13th Mercury enters Capricorn

This is a time when your words can climb to the top of the marketplace and bring you a great accomplishment. Write in your blog, take it out to a bigger marketplace, or send your words to a publisher. Your words will bring you wealth.

December 19th Venus goes retrograde in Capricorn

Prepare for brat attacks. Make sure that you do your holiday shopping early! Otherwise, you will buy everything for yourself and not have any leftover for family and others.

December 21st The Sun enters Capricorn

Personal recognition will become an issue. Time for a raise, a bonus, or a new job. Remember to acknowledge yourself for how far you have come.

December 28th Jupiter enters Pisces

Time to allow the good graces of Jupiter to reward you. This can be a magical time when the flow of good fortune works in your favor. Let it BE!

Super Sensitivity December 5th-6th, 12th-14th, and 19th-20th

This is a time to stay within your own boundaries. Think twice before you speak and all will be well!

Low Vitality December 17th-18th

Do not push the envelope. If you do, you will exhaust yourself.

Happy New Year and on to the Year of Love, 2022!

SUNDAY	MONDAY	TUESDAY	WEDNESDAY	THURSDAY	FRIDAY	SATURDAY
			1 ♅℞ ☽→♏ 3:55 AM ♆S/D 20° ♓ 24' 5:23 AM 3. Do what brings you joy.	**2** ♅℞ ☽ V/C 9:22 PM 4. Be a unifying presence.	**3** ♅℞ ☽→♐ 4:13 AM **Solar Eclipse** 12° ♐ 16' 11:33 PM ● 12° ♐ 22' 11:43 PM 5. Update an old tradition.	**4** ♅℞ ☽ V/C 9:07 PM 6. Music nurtures the soul.
5 ♅℞▲ ☽→♑ 3:31 AM 7. Stop and think before you speak.	**6** ♅℞▲ **Chanukah Ends at Nightfall** ☽ V/C 8:41 PM 8. It's okay to ask for more.	**7** ♅℞ ☽→♒ 3:49 AM 9. Donate your time or money.	**8** ♅℞ 10. A completion is also a beginning.	**9** ♅℞ ☽ V/C 1:59 AM ☽→♓ 6:54 AM 2. Decisions are easy, trust yourself.	**10** ♅℞ 3. Create a fun day.	**11** ♅℞ ☽ V/C 11:39 AM ☽→♈ 1:46 PM 4. Be conscious of the holiday plan.
12 ♅℞▲ 5. Here's your chance to mix it up!	**13** ♅℞▲ ♂→♐ 1:53 AM ☿→♑ 9:52 AM ☽ V/C 6:51 PM 6. It's time to decorate.	**14** ♅℞▲ ☽→♉ 12:11 AM 7. Study a modern philosopher.	**15** ♅℞ 8. Buy some Santa gifts for a charity.	**16** ♅℞ ☽ V/C 8:08 AM ☽→♊ 12:43 PM 9. Meditate for the well-being of All.	**17** ♅℞▼ 10. Start looking at goals for 2022.	**18** ♅℞▼ ○ 27° ♊ 29' 8:36 PM ☽ V/C 10:01 PM 2. A day to gather facts.
19 ♀♅℞▲ ☽→♋ 1:42 AM ♀℞ 26° ♑ 29' 2:36 AM 3. Find joy in spontaneous moments.	**20** ♀♅℞▲ 4. Order makes the day easier.	**21** ♀♅℞ ☽ V/C 6:43 AM **Winter Solstice** ☉→♑ 7:59 AM ☽→♌ 1:54 PM 5. Adaptability creates many options.	**22** ♀♅℞ 6. Stop, breathe in loving harmony.	**23** ♀♅℞ ☽ V/C 10:39 PM 7. Problem-solving skills are valuable.	**24** ♀♅℞ ☽→♍ 12:25 AM 8. You are your own authority.	**25** ♀♅℞ **Christmas** 9. May all people be blessed.
26 ♀♅℞ **Kwanzaa** ☽ V/C 12:39 AM ☽→♎ 8:23 AM 10. Expect goals to expand and grow.	**27** ♀♅℞ 11. See the magic in the Universe.	**28** ♀♅℞ ☽ V/C 1:10 PM ☽→♏ 1:16 PM ♃→♓ 8:09 PM 3. Use your imagination today.	**29** ♀♅℞ 4. Structure may be required.	**30** ♀♅℞ ☽ V/C 9:09 AM ☽→♐ 3:08 PM 5. Take a drive to see nature's beauty.	**31** ♀♅℞ **New Year's Eve** 6. Invite some friends over.	

♈ Aries	♍ Virgo	♒ Aquarius	♀ Venus	♆ Neptune	V/C Void-of-Course	2. Balance	7. Learning
♉ Taurus	♎ Libra	♓ Pisces	♂ Mars	♇ Pluto	℞ Retrograde	3. Fun	8. Money
♊ Gemini	♏ Scorpio	☉ Sun	♃ Jupiter	→ Enters	S/D Stationary Direct	4. Structure	9. Spirituality
♋ Cancer	♐ Sagittarius	☽ Moon	♄ Saturn	● New Moon	▲ Super Sensitivity	5. Action	10. Visionary
♌ Leo	♑ Capricorn	☿ Mercury	♅ Uranus	○ Full Moon	▼ Low Vitality	6. Love	11. Completion

New Moon in Sagittarius

December 3rd, 11:43 PM

When the Sun is in Sagittarius

Now is the time for greater expansion of consciousness. Sagittarius is about exterminating all of the man-eating symbols of our illusions, harmful thoughts, inertia, prejudices, and superstitions that hide behind our excuses. It is truth time, so that the Soul Goal of the Sagittarius can come into being and direct its light toward greater aspiration. Questions to ask yourself at this time are: What is my goal for myself? What is my goal for my nation? What is my goal for humanity? All goals get stimulated during this time.

Sagittarius Goddess

On a July night in 2020 on a Portland street, Athena was invoked in the heart of a young woman despairing for the state of her community. Wielding her greatest power, she strode naked before her aggressors. A mantle of thousands of years of righteous anger and justice denied, carried effortlessly and laid bare for the world to witness. The pressure cracked open a woman's heart and out poured Athena's wisdom, beauty, power and protection; shaming those peppering the crowds with rubber bullets, teargas and flash bangs with stark contrast. Some saw a single woman, vulnerable and unprotected, but others recognized the Goddess Divine. Before the display of unwelcome military might, she sat down in a meditative stance that could be nothing less than the exact opposite of their combative intent. She even allowed the forces to take their shots, bloodying her feet. She danced before them, channeling Kali, Athena, Boudicca and countless fore mothers for whom justice was denied. We who saw beyond the physical scene felt the palpable presence of the Warrior Goddess. She appeared as a force-interrupter; a contradiction so extreme it exposed the irony of so-called "peace-keepers" dressed in full riot gear turned aggressors attacking citizen protesters asking for an end to violence. It was clear who held the power that night. She trusted her unconscious software and allowed the connection between her and Athena to be powerfully embodied. Athena asks you to accept the power of the moment. Where do you feel her rise up in you?

Build Your Altar

Colors   Deep purple, deep blue, turquoise

Numerology   5 – Update an old tradition

Tarot Card   Temperance – Blending physical and spiritual

Gemstones   Turquoise, lapis

Plant Remedy Madia – Seeing the target and hitting it

Fragrance   Magnolia – Expanded beauty

Moon Notes

New Moon   12° Sagittarius 22'
New Moons are about opening new pathways for prosperity.

Solar Eclipse   11:33 PM

Element
Fire – Igniting, dissolving, accelerating, cleansing, advancing awareness, impatience, leadership, passion, and vitality.

Statement   I Aim

Body   Thighs

Mind   Philosophical

Spirit   Inspiration

3rd House Moon   I Speak/I Aim

Umbrella Energy
How you get the word out and the message behind the words.

Choice Points
Action   Imminent Opportunities
Non-action   Killjoy

Sabian Symbol
The Great Pyramid And The Sphinx.

Potential
Ancient knowledge being revealed.

Sagittarius Victories & Challenges

Say all of the statements in this section out loud. Then, underline the phrase that means the most to you. Use the phrase as your affirmation for manifesting throughout this moon phase.

Destiny is in my favor today. I know, without a doubt, that I cannot make a wrong turn today. I access my blueprint to ensure perfect timing for all opportunities to be open to me today. I promise to be open to these opportunities, knowing full well that today is my day. I am on time and in time today. My destiny is here and working in my favor. I see all that is available to me today and claim my pathway to success. I pay attention to what comes my way today and know that it is an opening for good fortune to be my reality. I am ready to accept my good fortune now. All I have to do is move in the direction of my truth. I know that my truth is my good fortune. I trust in coincidence and synchronicity to provide me with direction to my destiny. All points of action lead me to my true expression. I can see clearly into my future today with great optimism. I intend it. I allow it. So be it. All is in Divine Order.

Mantra during this Time *(repeat this 10 times out loud)*

"My truth is my good fortune. My timing is perfect. I trust that all that comes to me today is in my highest and best good. I am open to optimism. The drum of destiny beats in my favor. So be it!"

Sagittarius Homework

Sagittarians manifest best through teaching, publishing and writing, travel, spiritual adventures, and as tour group leaders, airline and cruise ship personnel, evangelical ministers, philosophers, anthropologists, linguists, and translators.

The Sagittarius moon cycle creates a magnetic matrix that stimulates us to take direction towards becoming one with a goal and then sheds light on the path. In the ancient mystery schools, Sagittarius moons were used to set the stage for candidates to reach higher levels of awareness by inspiring their desire to reach a goal and then to step toward the goal. It is time now to become one with your goal.

Victory List

Acknowledge what you have overcome. Keep this list active during this moon cycle. Honoring victory allows you to accept success.

Tarot

Ask the question out loud, then draw a card. You may wish to draw it or paste a copy of it here. Then write down what you feel it might be telling you, in response to the question. Use the glossary in the appendix and record here anything about the card that captures your attention. You may wish to come back throughout the moon cycle to meditate or journal more on the card.

How is my spirit supporting my manifesting?

Manifesting List

This or something better than this comes to me in an easy and pleasurable way, for the good of all concerned. Thank you, Universe!

Sagittarius Manifesting Ideas

Now is the time to focus on manifesting truth, teaching and study, understanding advanced ideas, optimism and inspiration, bliss, goals, travel and adventure, and philosophy and culture.

New Moon in Sagittarius

Your Personal Moon Experience

Fill in the Cosmic Check-In page. Then look up the Moon in the chart below. Take note of the "I" statement on the outside of the wheel where the Moon is located. This is the house the Moon is in, and the statement gives you the atmospheric energy, or the "umbrella energy" of this moon phase. This becomes the first statement to use in your mantra. Then, the "I" statement that corresponds with the astrological sign the Moon is in becomes the second statement (see *Moon Notes* for this moon phase). Now, locate the same sign and degree in your personal Natal chart and make a note of the house this degree falls in. The statement that corresponds with this house becomes your third statement. Go back to the Cosmic Check-In page and circle the three statements from the charts and read what you wrote. This will give you an idea about what to expect from this moon phase on a personal level. There is a video class that shows you how to read your personal chart at www.BlueMoonAcademy.com, look for *How to Use the Moon Book*.

I Speak, I Aim, I _____.

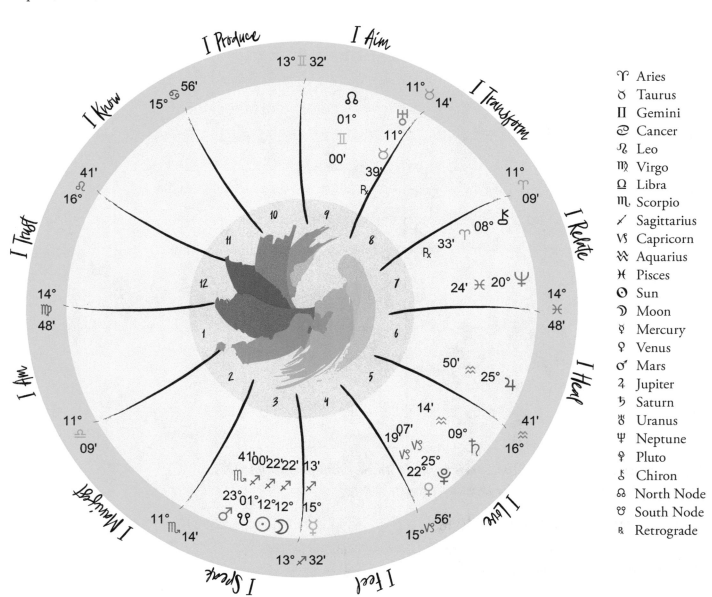

♈	Aries
♉	Taurus
♊	Gemini
♋	Cancer
♌	Leo
♍	Virgo
♎	Libra
♏	Scorpio
♐	Sagittarius
♑	Capricorn
♒	Aquarius
♓	Pisces
☉	Sun
☽	Moon
☿	Mercury
♀	Venus
♂	Mars
♃	Jupiter
♄	Saturn
♅	Uranus
♆	Neptune
♇	Pluto
⚷	Chiron
☊	North Node
☋	South Node
℞	Retrograde

Cosmic Check-In

Sagittarius New Moon
December 3rd, 11:43 PM

Take a moment to write a brief phrase for each "I" statement. This activates all areas of your life for this creative cycle.

♐ I Aim

♑ I Produce

♒ I Know

♓ I Trust

♈ I Am

♉ I Manifest

♊ I Speak

♋ I Feel

♌ I Love

♍ I Heal

♎ I Relate

♏ I Transform

Full Moon in Gemini

December 18th, 8:36 PM

When the Sun is Opposite the Moon

Full moons are always in opposition to the Sun. This creates a feeling of tension between where you want to shine and how your feelings are flowing on a sensory level about the Sun's directive. The two forces seem like they are working against each other, yet they are on the same team displaying different techniques to obtain the same mission. The Gemini/Sagittarius polarity creates tension between community ideas and global thinking.

Gemini Goddess

Some of Zeus's favorite consorts were the nymphs who lived on Mount Kithairon. One nymph in particular, Echo, incurred Zeus's wife Hera's wrath by trying to keep Zeus's philandering a secret. As a punishment, Hera cursed Echo with only being able to speak the last few words spoken to her. Echo was in love with Narcissus, but she was unable to tell him by speaking her own truth. As his own words were "echoed" back to him Narcissus fell in love with himself. It is said that after Narcissus died, Echo physically wasted away, until there was nothing left of her but the sound of her voice.

This new moon n Gemini pay attention to your communications. You have an opportunity to speak your own truth, unlike Echo. She would tell you that the power of your voice is not to be taken for granted. Your voice, your truth, can be your most important tool. Cherish it. Use it wisely. Listen to yourself as you speak. What do you say about yourself to yourself? What reverberates and repeats? Is it useful, is it kind, does it empower you, is it your truth? Many of us have "echoes" of childhood abuse in our heads. Allow Echo assist you to put a stop to your own inner abuse. Set yourself free from old echoes of the past. Replace the old words with kind mantras and paste them up on your mirror. Say the mantra daily until it becomes your reality.

Build Your Altar

Colors	Bright yellow, orange, multi-colors
Numerology	2 – A day to gather facts
Tarot Card	Lovers – Connecting to wholeness
Gemstones	Yellow diamond, citrine, yellow jade, yellow topaz
Plant remedy	Morning Glory – Thinking with your heart, not your head
Fragrance	Iris – The ability to focus the mind

Moon Notes

Full Moon 27° Gemini 29'
Full Moons are about moving beyond blocks and setting yourself free.

Element
Air – The breath of life that allows the mind to achieve new insights and fresh perspectives, abstract dreaming, freedom from attachments, codes of intelligence, and academic applications.

Statement I Speak

Body Lungs and Hands

Mind Academic

Spirit Messenger

11th House Moon I Know/I Speak

Umbrella Energy
Your approach to friends, social consciousness, teamwork, community service, and the future.

Choice Points
Action   Living in the Moment
Non-action   Aimless

Sabian Symbol
Through Bankruptcy, Society Gives To An Overburdened Individual The Opportunity To Begin Again.

Potential
Acceptance to begin again.

Clearing the Slate

Sixty hours before the full moon negative traits connected to the astro-sign might become activated to trigger what needs to be released during the full moon phase. You may notice that you are not listening to others and overriding what others are saying by talking too much. Watch out for gossiping or omitting the truth. Make a list, look in the mirror, and for each negative trait, tell yourself *I am sorry, I forgive you, thank you for your awareness,* and *I love you.* Now is the time to start doing your Sky Power Yoga poses so your physiology can feel supported during this moon phase. The poses and the teaching are available on BlueMoonAcademy.com.

Gemini Victories & Challenges

Say all of the statements in this section out loud. Then, underline the phrase that means the most to you. Use the phrase as your affirmation for releasing throughout this moon phase.

Today, I blend my old self with my new self, my physical reality with my spiritual awareness, my positive thoughts with my negative thoughts, my past with my present, my feminine with my masculine, my rewards with my losses, my ups with my downs, and my higher self with my lower self. It is a day for me to refine and fine tune my life by looking at my extremes. I recognize what inspires me and what keeps me stuck. I find my center today by acknowledging my extremes. I am aware that balance comes to those who are able to locate the space in the center of these opposite energy fields.

When I am in my center, my polarities are in motion. Healing cannot occur unless my polarities are moving and I know that healing is motion. I am ready for a healing today. I know that by visiting my opposites, and determining their vast opposition to each other, I can find the paradoxes that I have chosen for myself and begin to heal. I am willing to experiment with this blending of opposites and become the alchemist of my own life. When I blend all aspects of myself, rather than separating them, I can truly become whole. Today is a day to integrate, rather than separate, in order to release the spark of light that stays prisoner when my polarities are in operation. When I find balance, motion occurs and the Law of Harmony takes over, putting paradoxical energies to rest, thus breaking the crystallization of polarity. The Law of Harmony is beauty in motion and promotes the flow of color, light, sound, and movement into form. Balance is a condition that keeps my spark in motion. I become the vertical line in the center of polarity today and carry the secret of balance. Balance cannot be my goal; motion is my goal today. When I am in motion, I can take action to evolve and to express all of myself freely.

Gemini Homework

Sit still and invite silence into your space. Stay quiet and still for at least 5 minutes. During this time take an inventory and see where you have interrupted people in the middle of their sentences. Now is the time to make a conscious effort to allow others the space to express their thoughts. Keep sitting in silence and feel the frustration, while embracing the power of silence.

Gratitude List

Keep this list active throughout the moon cycle. This will bring you to a level of completion so that a new cycle of opportunity can occur in your life. Be prepared for miracles!

Tarot

Ask the question out loud, then draw a card. You may wish to draw it or paste a copy of it here. Then write down what you feel it might be telling you, in response to the question. Use the glossary in the appendix and record here anything about the card that captures your attention. You may wish to come back throughout the moon cycle to meditate or journal more on the card.

How is my mind supporting my releasing?

Releasing List

Say this statement out loud three times before writing your list:

I am a free spiritual being and it is my desire to be free to think and to express myself fully.

From this day forward I resolve to be true — first to myself and my highest self, and then to the highest self in me which is the Source of Love That I Am.

Gemini Releasing Ideas

Now is the time to activate a game change in my life, and give up my attitude about unfinished business, shallow communication, old files and office clutter, broken communication devices, lies I tell myself, temptation to gossip, restlessness, over-thinking, and vacillation.

Full Moon in Gemini

Your Personal Moon Experience

Fill in the Cosmic Check-In page. Then look up the Moon in the chart below. Take note of the "I" statement on the outside of the wheel where the Moon is located. This is the house the Moon is in, and the statement gives you the atmospheric energy, or the "umbrella energy" of this moon phase. This becomes the first statement to use in your mantra. Then, the "I" statement that corresponds with the astrological sign the Moon is in becomes the second statement (see *Moon Notes* for this moon phase). Now, locate the same sign and degree in your personal Natal chart and make a note of the house this degree falls in. The statement that corresponds with this house becomes your third statement. Go back to the Cosmic Check-In page and circle the three statements from the charts and read what you wrote. This will give you an idea about what to expect from this moon phase on a personal level. There is a video class that shows you how to read your personal chart at www.BlueMoonAcademy.com, look for *How to Use the Moon Book*.

I Know, I Speak, I _____ .

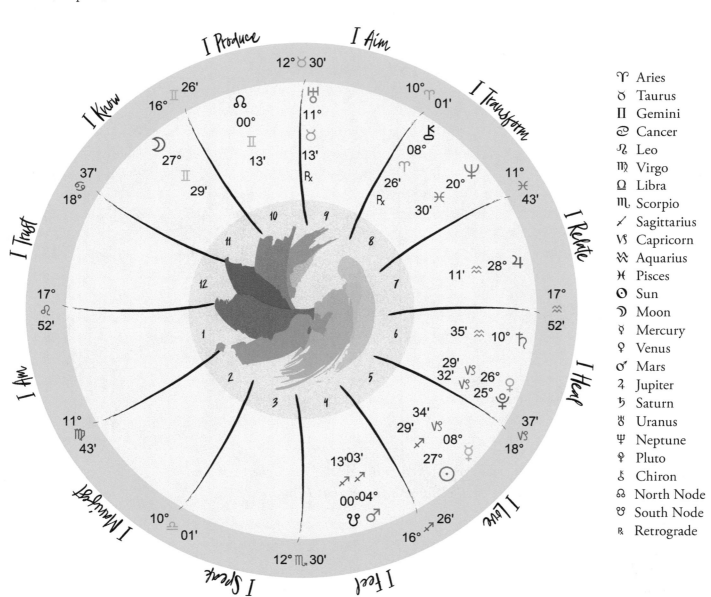

♈	Aries
♉	Taurus
♊	Gemini
♋	Cancer
♌	Leo
♍	Virgo
♎	Libra
♏	Scorpio
♐	Sagittarius
♑	Capricorn
♒	Aquarius
♓	Pisces
☉	Sun
☽	Moon
☿	Mercury
♀	Venus
♂	Mars
♃	Jupiter
♄	Saturn
♅	Uranus
♆	Neptune
♇	Pluto
⚷	Chiron
☊	North Node
☋	South Node
℞	Retrograde

Cosmic Check-In

Gemini Full Moon
December 18th, 8:36 PM

Take a moment to write a brief phrase for each "I" statement. This activates all areas of your life for this creative cycle.

♊ I Speak

♋ I Feel

♌ I Love

♍ I Heal

♎ I Relate

♏ I Transform

♐ I Aim

♑ I Produce

♒ I Know

♓ I Trust

♈ I Am

♉ I Manifest

Appendices

Eclipses

Lunar	May 26th	✗	Sagittarius
Solar	June 10th	Ⅱ	Gemini
Lunar	November 19th	♉	Taurus
Solar	December 3rd	✗	Sagittarius

Retrogrades

	BEGINS			ENDS		
Uranus	August 15th, 2020	♉	Taurus	January 14th, 2021		
Mercury	January 30th	♒	Aquarius	February 20th		
Pluto	April 27th	♑	Capricorn	October 6th		
Saturn	May 23rd	♒	Aquarius	October 10th		
Mercury	May 29th	Ⅱ	Gemini	June 22nd		
Jupiter	June 20th	♓	Pisces	October 17th	♒	Aquarius
Neptune	June 25th	♓	Pisces	December 1st		
Uranus	August 19th	♉	Taurus	January 18th, 2022		
Mercury	September 27th	♎	Libra	October 18th		
Venus	December 19th	♑	Capricorn	January 29th, 2022		

Tibetan Numerology of the Day

2	**Balance**	Be decisive and move past vacillation.
3	**Fun**	Have a party. Take on a creative project. Express the "Disneyland" side of yourself.
4	**Structure**	Take the day to organize. Get the job done. Work and you will sail through the day.
5	**Action, exercise, travel**	Exercise—join a gym, take a dance class, play tennis, go for a walk. Travel—go for a drive, travel the world, visit your travel agent. Make a change.
6	**Love**	Go out for a night of romance. Work on beauty in your home. Nurture yourself and take care of your health.
7	**Research**	Read a book. Learn something new and get smart. Take a class.
8	**Money**	Have a business meeting. Meet with your accountant. Make a sales call. Start a new business.
9	**Connecting with the Divine**	Meditate. Take part in a humanitarian project. Do community service.
10	**Seeing the "big picture"**	Take an innovative idea and run with it today!
11	**Completion**	Do what it takes to be complete.

The Astro Wheel

	STATEMENT	RULING SIGN		KEY NOTES
1st House	**I Am**	♈	Aries	Your outer appearance, the way you present yourself, the way you dress, the way you enter a room, and what you leave behind when you leave the room.
2nd House	**I Manifest**	♉	Taurus	The way you make your money and the way you spend your money.
3rd House	**I Speak**	♊	Gemini	How you get the word out and the message behind the words.
4th House	**I Feel**	♋	Cancer	The way your early environmental training was and how that set your foundation for living, and why you chose your mother.
5th House	**I Love**	♌	Leo	The way you love and how you want to be loved.
6th House	**I Heal**	♍	Virgo	The way you manage your body and its appearance.
7th House	**I Relate**	♎	Libra	One-on-one relationships, defines your people attraction, and how you work in relationships with the people you attract.
8th House	**I Transform**	♏	Scorpio	How you share money and other resources, what you keep hidden regarding sex, death, real estate, and regeneration.
9th House	**I Aim**	♐	Sagittarius	The way you approach spirituality, philosophy, journeys, higher knowledge, and aspiration.
10th House	**I Produce**	♑	Capricorn	Your approach to status, career, honor, and prestige, and why you chose your father.
11th House	**I Know**	♒	Aquarius	Your approach to friends, social consciousness, teamwork, community service, and the future.
12th House	**I Trust**	♓	Pisces	Determines how you deal with your karma, "unconscious software," and what you will experience in order to attain mastery to complete your karma. It is also about the way you connect to the Divine.

Heavenly Bodies

☉	**Sun**	Outer personality, potential, director, the most obvious traits of the consciousness projection
☽	**Moon**	Emotion, feelings, memory, unconsciousness, mother's influence, ancestors, home life
☿	**Mercury**	The way you think, the intention beneath your thoughts, communication, academia (lower mind)
♀	**Venus**	Beauty, value, romantic love, sensuality, creativity, being social, fun, femininity
♂	**Mars**	Action, change, variety, sex drive, ambition, warrior, ego, athletics, masculinity
♃	**Jupiter**	Benevolent, jovial, excessive, expansive, optimistic, abundant, extravagant, accepting good fortune
♄	**Saturn**	Teacher, karma, disciplined, restrictive, father's influence
♅	**Uranus**	Liberated, revolutionary, explosive, spontaneous, breakthrough, innovation, technology
♆	**Neptune**	Mystical, charming, sensitive, addictive, glamorous, deceptive, illusions
♇	**Pluto**	Money, wealth, transformation, secrets, hidden information, sexuality, psychic power
⚷	**Chiron**	Wounded healer, healing, holistic therapies
☊	**North Node**	This represents where you are headed in this lifetime. In other words, it represents the direction your life will take you, your future focus. In Eastern astrology, this is sometimes called the "head of the dragon."
☋	**South Node**	This represents what you brought with you this lifetime and what you are moving away from. It is sometimes called the "tail of the dragon" in Eastern astrology.

Astrological Signs

Each sign of astrology has a particular quality or tone that is described in more detail with the moons.

Sign	"I" Statement		Element	Key Words
♈ **Aries**	I Am	Sign of the Ram Ruled by Mars ♂ Begins the zodiac year with the Spring Equinox	Fire	Ego, identity, championship, leadership, action-oriented, warrior, and self-first.
♉ **Taurus**	I Manifest	Sign of the Bull Ruled by Venus ♀	Earth	Self-value, abundant, aesthetic, business, sensuous, art, beauty, flowers, gardens, collector, and shopper.
♊ **Gemini**	I Speak	Sign of the Twins Ruled by Mercury ☿	Air	Versatile, expressive, restless, travel-minded, short trips, flirt, gossip, "nose for news," and the messenger.
♋ **Cancer**	I Feel	Sign of the Crab Ruled by the Moon ☽ Begins with the Summer Solstice	Water	Emotional, nurturing, family-oriented, home, mother, cooking, security-minded, ancestors, builder of form and foundation.
♌ **Leo**	I Love	Sign of the Lion Ruled by the Sun ☉	Fire	Willful, dramatic, loyal, children, child-ego state, love affairs, decadent, royal, show-stopper, theatre, adored and adoring.
♍ **Virgo**	I Heal	Sign of the Virgin Ruled by Mercury ☿	Earth	Gives birth to Divinity, perfectionist, discernment, scientific, analytical, habitual, work-oriented, body maintenance, earth connection, attention to detail, service-oriented, earth healer, herbs, and judgmental.
♎ **Libra**	I Relate	Sign of the Scales Ruled by Venus ♀ Begins with the Autumnal Equinox	Air	Relationship, social, harmony, industry, the law, diplomacy, morality, beauty, strategist, logical, and over-active mind.
♏ **Scorpio**	I Transform	Sign of the Scorpion Ruled by Pluto ♀ and Mars ♂	Water	Intense, passionate, sexual, powerful, focused, controlling, deep, driven, and secretive.
♐ **Sagittarius**	I Aim	Sign of the Archer Ruled by Jupiter ♃	Fire	Optimistic, generous, preacher-teacher, world traveler, higher knowledge, goal-oriented, philosophy, culture, publishing, extravagance, excessive, exaggerator, and good fortune.
♑ **Capricorn**	I Produce	Sign of the Goat Ruled by Saturn ♄ Begins at the Winter Solstice	Earth	Ambitious, concretive, responsible, achievement, business, corporate structure, world systems, and useful.
♒ **Aquarius**	I Know	Sign of the Water Bearer Ruled by Uranus ♅	Air	Inventive, idealistic, utopian, rebellion, innovative, technology, community, friends, synergy, group consciousness, science, magic, trendy, and future-orientation.
♓ **Pisces**	I Trust	Sign of the Fishes Ruled by Neptune ♆	Water	Sensitive, creative, empathetic, theatre, addiction, escape artist, glamor, secretive, Divinely guided, healer, medicine.

Colors

- **Red** — Passion, bloodline, circulation, ancestry
- **Pink** — Shy passion, learning to stand up for yourself, unconditional love, timid, colors in between the vertebrae of the spinal cord teaching you to stand up yourself
- **Orange** — Money, sex, power, creativity, Christ healer, integration of the physical at a deeper level
- **Yellow** — Enlightenment, a bright mind (perhaps too logical), happiness, joy, playful, higher mind, purist form of logic, the Sun
- **Green** — Natural, nature, envy, abundance, heart, go
- **Turquoise** — Sky power, spontaneous, futuristic, innovative
- **Blue** — Third-eye perception, moody, water, the flow of emotion, depth, psychic, fantasy, throat, communication, emotional body
- **Indigo** — Absence of guilt, opening to aspects of the future, creating new pathways
- **Violet** — Magical thinking, abstract thinking, abstract mind, guilt-ridden
- **Purple** — Ego, royalty, controlling version of power
- **Rainbow** — Indicates a good future, open to all possibilities
- **Gold** — Personal value, self worth, valuable
- **Silver** — Intuition, reflective, ability to see yourself, the Moon
- **White** — Major change, includes all colors
- **Clear** — Clarity, cleaning, getting it clear, no color
- **Black** — Intuitive, receptive, emptiness, absence of color, inner self, the void

Tarot Glossary

A Universal Support System: The Major Arcana Cards

The first 22 cards in the deck, numbered with Roman numerals 0-21, are the most potent cards in the deck and are a model of wholeness. Each Major Arcana card singles out a stage of development on the spectrum of wholeness. Each has a law (shown in capital letters) and a lesson reflecting the values of our times and promoting the evolution of experience on the internal and external planes of awareness. The law is what you have to learn while traveling here. The lesson is the experience which allows the law to be learned.

Reversals

After drawing a card, turn it over side-to-side, like a page in a book. Reversals are cards that are upside-down to you as you read the cards. This is true whether you are reading for yourself or for someone else since the cards are always laid out for the reader, the person interpreting the cards. The qualities listed under the Reversed heading are merely showing you the inner place and inner work that is needed in your development.

THE FOOL – 0

POTENTIAL. The promise of things to come. The energy you are bringing into yourself in the moment. A leap of faith. A new beginning. A go-for-it attitude. Accessing your potential (not caring if you look foolish). Remember, the guy with the lamp shade on his head may be having more fun than you. Willing to play full out. Going through life lightheartedly.

REVERSED: Unwilling to take risks. No faith in yourself. Worry. Holding yourself back. Being afraid of looking foolish. Afraid to let go and "let God." No faith to take the leap. Taking life too seriously.

THE MAGICIAN – I

TALENT. Ability to convert from the ethereal to the physical. Masculine polarity in its purest form. All things are possible for you. Having all the tools for success. Time to focus your intention and attention. A man who symbolizes every fantasy.

REVERSED: Misuse of power. A master of illusion. Seeing everything as impossible. Lacking self-confidence. Doubting your ability to manifest or create. Not accessing your tools (talent).

THE HIGH PRIESTESS – II

INTUITION. The Feminine polarity in its purest form. Purity, the Virgin Goddess within. A woman who symbolizes every fantasy. Dispenser of wisdom and knowledge.

REVERSED: Not trusting your intuition. Overriding intuition with logic. Diluting your femininity. Prostituting yourself. Selling yourself short. Time to ask, "What intuitive hit am I not listening to?"

THE EMPRESS – III

LOVE. The epitome of the Natural Woman. Fertility. Nurturance. The ability to get your needs met. Flowing with what feels natural. Knowing how to take care of yourself and others. Being touchable, lovable and nurturing. The perfect wife/mother. Creativity at its best.

REVERSED: Not nurturing self or others. A poor self-image manifests in feeling unloved. Ask, what it is you want in order to get your needs met. Do for yourself rather than expect others to do for you. Remember, you can only be loved to the extent you love yourself.

THE EMPEROR – IV

SUCCESS. Ability to respond to success and manifest in the outside world. The perfect husband/father. Successful in business. Structured, logical and grounded. Having a foundation for success. Chairman of the Board type.

REVERSED: Not assuming responsibility – in the world, in a relationship, in business. Disorganized. A social dropout. Unable to work the system for success in the world. Disconnected. Rebellious against the system. A man who has turned his back on a woman.

THE HIEROPHANT – V

TRADITION. The authority figure. The bridge between humanity and divinity. The teacher's teacher. The interpreter of life (teacher, lawyer, therapist, preacher, rabbi, doctor) through listening and reflection. Seeking interpretation through traditions, social awareness, church, dogma, society's rules. Needing advise and interpretation through the eyes of an authority.

REVERSED: Learning to interpret life for yourself. Breaking away from tradition, dogma, ritual, church, society's rules. Learning to live by using your own intuition and becoming your own authority. Knowing there is more to life than what meets the eye. Seeing beyond the physical.

THE LOVERS – VI

RELATIONSHIP. Integration of the masculine and feminine life energy. Perfect inner balance of the masculine and feminine principles. Union of opposites. Healthy relationship. Commitment. Marriage. Good health.

REVERSED: Broken partnerships. Selfishness. Love for all the wrong reasons. Divorce. Separation. Bad health. Lack of commitment. Disharmony.

THE CHARIOT – VII

ACTION. Taking action for victory in life. Broad, sweeping changes. Positioning yourself for success. Take action now to move forward in life.

REVERSED: Upheaval in your life from not taking action. Putting your foot on the brakes when it needs to be on the gas pedal. Chaos.

STRENGTH – VIII

PASSION. Understanding the dynamics of the beauty and the beast within. Learning to express your higher and lower selves without judgment. Integrating consciousness with the physical, thereby creating a passion for life.

REVERSED: Denial of natural expression. Giving power away to your lower forces. Out of control. Stubborn. Lacking courage. Health issues. Exhaustion.

THE HERMIT – IX

INDIVIDUALITY. Knowing ourselves as an individuals. Recognize your inner qualities. Your God-self uniqueness manifests your inner light. Time to take your spirituality off the mountaintop and shine your light out into the world.

REVERSED: Contemplating and observing. Hiding out and retreating from life. Denying your own individuality. Not sharing your knowledge; keeping it to yourself. Caution: Do not stay on the mountaintop too long.

THE WHEEL OF FORTUNE – X

LIFE LESSON. In time and on time with your life's blueprint. The drum of destiny beats in your favor. Applying the knowledge of your life lessons and experiencing good fortune. Being in the right time at the right place to experience what appears to be a miracle.

REVERSED: Denying your destiny. Taken off your path. Everything out of sync. Denial of life lessons. Getting stuck in feeling sorry for yourself. Misfortune.

JUSTICE – XI

KARMA. Activating the laws of Cause and Effect. (Every action has a reaction; what you put out you get back.) Expect compensation for actions taken. Actions now get equalized and balanced. Winning a lawsuit. Reaping benefits.

REVERSED: Not accepting responsibility for your actions. Being forced to face what you do not want to see. Blaming others rather than seeing the balance of action. Feeling as if an injustice has been done.

THE HANGED MAN – XII

DETACHMENT. Learning to accept rather than control. Taking time out to reflect. Being willing to "hang out" and do nothing. Being calm in the midst of the storm.

REVERSED: Clinging to the past. Living life through a rear view mirror. Not willing to change. Afraid to just hang out and observe. Trying to control. Being a martyr.

DEATH – XIII

TRANSFORMATION. There is no compromise – change is imminent. Make a clean break. Time to let go of the past. Rejuvenation. Regeneration. New beginnings.

REVERSED: The Universe has you on hold. Delays are appropriate. Do not personalize the feeling of "stuckness." Take time to play rather than pushing. Let go of what you think the action "should" be. Be willing to stay in the void.

TEMPERANCE – XIV

BALANCE. Experimentation and modification. This is a time of learning to manage life by blending extremes, knowing boundaries and setting limits. Inner and outer congruity is very important now. Know what it takes to keep yourself centered.

REVERSED: Life is unmanageable. Moderation is needed. Obsessive and compulsive behaviors are causing imbalance. Could indicate poor health, exhaustion, stress. Out of alignment with spiritual and physical realities. Time to set limits and boundaries.

THE DEVIL – XV

CONFINEMENT. Feeling confined, constricted, limited. 360-degree test with 180-degree vision. Options required. Ask yourself, how many different ways can I look at this situation.

REVERSED: The light at the end of the tunnel appears. The testing period is over. The road to freedom has been found. You have seen your options. The solution to your problem has been found.

THE TOWER – XVI

SPONTANEITY. Learning to live in the moment. An unexpected event leads you into freedom. Do not put anything off until tomorrow. Do whatever is appropriate in the moment. Clear the way so new consciousness can appear.

REVERSED: Resisting change. Staying stuck by trying to control the outcome. Refusing to go with the flow. A blessing in disguise.

THE STAR – XVII

NEW DIRECTIONS. Breakthrough to a new level of consciousness. On track. Golden opportunities on the horizon. Support coming from higher sources to provide guidance and direction.

REVERSED: Search for inner direction rather than outer guideposts. A missed opportunity. Time to ask, "Where am I being thrown off course and not willing to accept a new level of consciousness?"

THE MOON – XVIII

FEARS AND PHOBIAS. A time to face up to and look at what you keep hidden from yourself. A warning to stay on the path and avoid outside influences of negativity. Being deceived or deceiving yourself. Absorbing toxic or poisonous energy; i.e., drugs or alcohol. Drug or alcohol abuse. Time to face your darker side and bring it into the light.

REVERSED: A warning of personal safety. Danger in the dark. Doing anything to avoid facing the truth. Secrets, lies, deception, depression and repression. Denial, cheating, illegal activities.

THE SUN – XIX

ENLIGHTENMENT. The source of energy, happiness, abundance, success, prosperity, fulfillment, playfulness. The child-ego state revealed.

REVERSED: Not seeing that all is available to you. Where you are denying yourself happiness? Your dimmer switch is turning down the sunlight!

JUDGEMENT – XX

FREEDOM. Freedom from judgement. A clean slate is now available, a new life on a new level of consciousness. Congratulations! You have let go and integrated beyond black/white, right/wrong, good/bad and have moved into a more integrated version of yourself.

REVERSED: Being your own worst enemy, judging yourself constantly, beating yourself up, making yourself wrong, afraid of what people think, feeling guilty. Low self-esteem. Stop punishing yourself for past deeds and let go.

THE WORLD – XXI

ATTAINMENT. Unlimited opportunity for success. Attainment. Having it all. Your full potential realized. Victory in life. Mastery of the inner and outer planes of awareness. Acknowledge your accomplishments.

REVERSED: Fear of failure. Not willing to take responsibility for success. A loser attitude. Never bringing anything to completion. Feeling defeated. Walking to the door of success and saying, "Oh well, it wouldn't have worked, anyway."

About the Author

Beatrex Quntanna

Tarot expert, published author, symbolist, poet, lecturer—Beatrex is one of the luminaries of our time. Synthesizing 45 years of spiritual teachings, intuitive skills, and conventional counseling, she translates this wealth of wisdom into practical language making it accessible to all and applicable in today's world. Known for being "the teacher's teacher," her experience and advice has served as an invaluable support for many of today's spiritual teachers and professional psychics. She guides with profound insight, compassion for the human experience, and humor; inspiring personal growth and activating an inner-knowing in her students that sparks a self-confidence to walk tall in this world as a spiritual being.

Her life's work is showing how to Live Love Every Day by *living* astrology, not just intellectualizing it—teaching others how to ebb and flow with the natural cycles of the Moon and the cosmos, rather than working against them. She teaches this through Moon Classes held regularly throughout the year, and is the creator of *Living by the Light of the Moon*, a popular annual workbook that takes you step-by-step through her process.

The ultimate book on the Tarot and its symbols, *Tarot: A Universal Language* by Beatrex Quntanna, has been reviewed by magazines in Europe as well as in the United States. Her expertise in symbolism and Numerology, as well as her extraordinary psychic insight, make this book unique among Tarot books.

Beatrex also creates jewelry that heals and enlivens, *Spirituality on a String*. More than just necklaces and accessories, these are power pieces you will want to wear every day. She strings every bead by hand, with love, drawing from her vast collection of unique and hard-to-find pendants and beads from Tibet, Nepal, India, and the Far East.

Most recently she was gifted an online school from Melinda Pajak, called Blue Moon Academy. With the help of her production team Beatrex has used it to develop her own online courses, and has been working with teachers from around the country to produce content for the Academy. This includes turning Sky Power Yoga, a collaboration with Yoga teacher Jennifer Vause, into an ongoing video class series.

Beatrex's many print credits, as well as numerous radio, TV, and video appearances include:

- Contributing author to two anthologies by Maria Yracébûrû – *Prophetic Voices* and *Ah-Kine Remembrance*
- *How to Use the Moon Book* online video course produced by Blue Moon Academy
- *Tarot: A Universal Language* online course produced by Blue Moon Academy
- *Tibetan Numerology* online course produced by Blue Moon Academy

Beatrex continues to teach online Astrology and Tarot classes worldwide. She resides in Encinitas, California.

Interested in Ongoing Moon Classes and workshops with Beatrex?

Contact her at beatrex@cox.net
or visit **www.Beatrex.com**

Online Classes

Sky Power Yoga

Welcome to the "Moon Book" in motion!

It's important to have your physiology supported and connected to the Astrology as it becomes magnetized by each full and new moon. Yoga has contributed to the body for centuries as it defines a spiritual anatomy through the geometric forms known as the chakras. Sky Power Yoga is designed to awaken the body and connect it to the sky during each moon phase with combinations of easy poses and mantras.

Sky Power Yoga has been illustrated in the "Moon Book" for the last three years, and the process has been refined every year. Now we want to share it as an ongoing video series that will be available each month to support you.

Jennifer Vause, R.Y.T., our Yoga facilitator and co-creator of Sky Power Yoga, did her teacher training through the Soul of Yoga in Encinitas, California. The Soul of Yoga was one of the earliest yoga training facilities in the west (USA versus India). She has been teaching gentle and restorative yoga classes at the Soul of Yoga for about 8 years.

This monthly subscription course includes:

- Instructional videos customized to every moon cycle.
- Notification as each new class becomes available to you.

Enroll Today:
www.SkyPowerYoga.com

Online Classes with Beatrex

How to Use the Moon Book

Everything you need to know about using the *Living by the Light of the Moon* workbook to create magic and abundance in your life!

How to navigate your life by the light of the Moon and its cycles, this annual workbook—also known to Beatrex's students as "The Moon Book"—will show you step-by-step when and what to do to release whatever holds you back, and when and what to do to manifest what you truly want in your life.

Following along with this video class series helps you understand how to use the workbook easily and effortlessly.

The course includes:

- High-quality instructional videos on each aspect of the book.
- A handout that makes it easy to follow along.
- And the warmth and wisdom of Beatrex to carry you on your journey.

For more information or to enroll now go to www.BlueMoonAcademy.com

---

Tarot: A Universal Language

Experience the amazing interpretation and wisdom behind each and every Tarot card from Beatrex. This course is now available online for the first time ever. Beatrex has over forty-three years of experience giving Tarot readings and teaching the Tarot to her students.

Now this wealth of knowledge is available to you to study at your leisure.

In this online course you will...

- Get to know the meanings and symbols of the Tarot cards.
- Understand how to increase your intuition by using the cards.
- Receive special reading spreads appropriate for different issues.
- Meditate with the cards—let the symbols speak to you.
- Learn how to set up a vortex in your office for doing readings.
- Understand how to care for and treat your Tarot deck.

The course includes high-quality instructional videos, study aids, fun quizzes, and insightful activities. Whether you are on a journey to learn the Tarot for your own enlightenment or whether you want to do Tarot card readings for others, this is the course for you. Beatrex fills the course with her insightful wisdom, funny stories, and deep, anchored knowledge of the Tarot. Don't miss this course.

For more information or to enroll now go to www.BlueMoonAcademy.com

Other Publications by Beatrex

2021 The Year of Adaptability – Wall Calendar

Created by Beatrex Quntanna

Numerology by Michelenne Crab
Art and Design by Jennifer Masters

Live by Cycles Instead of by Time

This is the calendar from Beatrex's *Living by the Light of the Moon* workbook as a stand-alone work of art—for your home, your office, or a gift for someone special—putting all of Beatrex's information at your fingertips as a quick and easy reference to guide you day by day!

To order, go to www.Beatrex.com
or call 1-760-944-6020

Tarot: A Universal Language

By Beatrex Quntanna

Experiencing the Road of Life Through Symbols

Embark on this fascinating journey through the unfolding Story of Life as told by the Universal Language of the Tarot. This book contains innovative avenues to understand the tarot through the author's in-depth knowledge of symbology.

Learn how to quickly read and interpret the Tarot by following this simple, informative, and illustrated guide. Use the expanded symbology section to understand each symbol depicted on the Minor and Major Arcana cards.

This book includes an interpretation of all 78 Tarot cards, plus readings created by this nationally-known Tarot teacher, reader, and symbolist.

To order, go to www.Beatrex.com
or call 1-760-944-6020

CPSIA information can be obtained
at www.ICGtesting.com
Printed in the USA
LVHW050342180121
676772LV00011B/377